A5$_2$

2nd compact collection of literary effusions

I0426545

Roscoe Forthright

roscoeforthright. com has ceased to exist.

all videos and the Literary Broadsheets
now live on www.amberriverwood.com

As an historical fact, the deletion of the
first website was caused by one angry
lesbian who felt it was her moral
obligation to create fear and trembling
in the hearts and minds of all the
beautiful, happy young women I have
had sex with. This appears to be normal
and acceptable behavior in Liberal,
socially sensitive, we-care-about-you
society in our 21st Century in the United
States of America.

Roscoe Forthright

Sept. 2021

ENTRY #1

Having two girls in your bed at the same time is not always a good idea. If they are young daughters of devout Mormons, and your bed is located in Salt Lake City, you are asking for trouble. And it will be your own stupid fault. It would be much safer for you to think fondly of your girls at a safe distance, and jack your jizz as frequently as needed.

On other occasions, in other places, with other girls, two is often more fun than one, especially when the girls are bisexual and enjoy each other just as much as you enjoy both of them! My playful friends, Amber, Beth, Rosalee and sometimes Bea, are happy when extra hands are available to reach all the right places at just the right time. So much relies on what expectations each person brings into the room. When no one is looking for extended commitments, or large quantities of cash, or making some other business deals, the potential for joyful pleasure increases exponentially. When warmth, tenderness and honest friendship fill the room...

there is no limited to amounts of shared joy and pleasure. Some people truly do not know how to do this. Some people want to control the people around them, or be subservient to other people. In other words, the rooms contains masters and slaves, rather than a group of equals. Grown-ups really should learn to act like grown-ups. This or that fantasy game is truly not as worthwhile, and has far less spiritual potential, than a room of grown-ups, loving each other and bringing each other joy, just because that is the most satisfying thing to do.

I do not fault BDSM or role-play of any kind as sexual entertainment, but I have found not spiritual growth there. Spiritual grown occurs when there is no fantasy at all. The room contains people who love each other, and are confident in that love, and allow that love to grow over time, and be sustained over weeks, months and years. In that room there is no sense of "ownership" or arbitrary exclusivity. Again, this kind of love-making is not for everyone. Some people honestly require and sense of ownership and exclusivity. To each their own.

In my life, I found limited forms of sexual behavior more annoying than valuable. Some people just can't wait to invent a new rule, or a new standard of conduct, or a new use of language to limit or contain wildly beautiful instincts...

innate instincts which have no need to be limited nor contained. Some people simply enjoy controlling other people, and use every available method to do so, to get their way. Often they never question the purpose or value of the "way" they are pushing, nor the various, nasty end results of pushing other people around.

As I have mentioned elsewhere, I prefer clear language, with no pushy agendas. Words like, "I wanna fuck you in the ass," are beautifully concise, detailing a specific plan of action. But, it might not include tenderness, love and the good sense of humor. When a pretty girl in the video holds the shiny butt-plug up to her lover, and says, "Put it in my ass." We could easily miss all the tenderness and anticipation and pent-up joy both humans feel. Perhaps they have been busy for days, aching over many nights, leading up to that one moment in time.

Not being in a hurry is one way to cause spiritual joy. For example: I look at picture of Beth on my cell-phone, various images of us together, or her naked with her dildo, or Beth and Eva naked together, or Beth, Eva, Rosalee and myself in bed together. I have clear memories of jacking-it, laying next to the girls, as they have casual conversation. At that moment, none being sexually aroused at all. I laugh at my own lust, and jack-it again looking at these images.

In my mind I repeat their names, like a mantra, know I honestly love and desire each woman, and knowing I will continue to love and desire each woman, for a long time. Probably until the day each one decides, for whatever reasons, to exit my life, and not look back. I am fully aware this may happen, and even expect it to happen. I have no wish for anyone to be present in my life, one moment longer than they wish to be. I want no servants of slaves of any kind. I want these women in my life and in my bed, only as long as that is where they wish to be.

ENTRY #2

I allow my own innate desire to raise the boats, as with the incoming tide. The girls float, each moored to their own way of life, and I have no intention to interfere with their way of life. I simply wish to lift the keel, give some room for motion. In simple words: I want Amber and Rosalee to suck my erection, to caress my balls as they suck my erection. I want Beth to play with herself, to ease a big dildo inside her, as the girls take turns sucking on me. Truly, this is not an unreasonable expectation. Three naked girls in a yurt, enjoying a warm September afternoon. Three girls fully aroused, helping each other get-off; helping me get-off.

If we are able, and in the mood, perhaps we will orgasm together. Four orgasms at the same time, each one of us waiting for the others, holding back until everyone in the yurt has reached an urgent moment of ecstasy. Hips will jolt and quiver; my happy fellow will spurt a geyser, a thick, sustained geyser! When all the people in the room love each other, when each one requires the joy of others to sustain their own joy, when four people orgasm together, spiritual evolution becomes possible. Grown-ups cause their own forward motion by deliberate choices and deliberate actions, by thoughtful improvements to their lives. I ask for nothing random, frivolous, arbitrary or irrelevant.

Mutual orgasms among two, three, and four people can create such an improvements. Beyond four, the scene becomes too confusing, more like a drunken orgy than a clear-headed religious experience.

The two experiences have very little in common, except human bodies in orgasm. The minds reside in entirely different realms. An orgy is not a religious experience. Shared orgasms, if done well, among grown-ups, can certainly be a religious experience. If you do not believe me, try it for yourselves. Get some trusted fuck-buddies together, with a stated goal of expanding your minds. Say this openly: "Hey, Tommy, let's get naked with Susie and Bill, and touch God. You can eat Susie's pussy as she sucks on Bill."

More ridiculous things have occurred between people. More ridiculous things have been tried as methods to make magick, to raise spiritual awareness and get closer to God. I am fully aware, spiritual Rule-Makers frown upon unauthorized excursions into Spiritual Realms, using unauthorized means. Most Rule-Makers are relentless makers of money, and are in the religion business specifically for that purpose. I have meet only a few alert and honest people, who make suggestions, and never call them rules. The suggestions are made as helpful precautions against violent forces, and truly evil forces, which exist.

We see these forces at work everyday, as polite, well-educated Senators and Congress-people vote to sell bombs and high-powered weapons to violent and distant countries. As if dead bodies far away carry no moral weight, as if those dead bodies do not matter, as if making money from the surplus weapons is all that truly matters. Our Liberal, humanist-talking leaders vote, and approve such arms deals almost every year. How much evil is compounded daily, by such polite talkers, and what is the actual value of their expensive educations at Harvard, Princeton, Yale and Stanford?

Evil means, creating suffering, or creating piles of dead bodies. Where the suffering occurs is not relevant to the moral weight. Far off, among unimportant people in unimportant countries, for unimportant reasons.... that is often how dead bodies pile up, dead bodies caused specifically by the deliberate choices of our own self-righteous leaders in the United States of America.

Have I strayed off topic? No. I was talking about tangible evil. And I offer only one clear example of national tangible evil. The smaller evils are done by aggressive people pushing other people around. It remains prudent to guard one's life against such demons. Especially so, when attempting the magick of group sex. Choose your partners with great care.

ENTRY #3

The problem of talented and original writers in the 21st century is an audience with sensory overload, and miles of unfiltered or obsessively filtered pages of the internet. Unlike a physical bookstore, the internet gets you places through "search" words, and search words as hopelessly imprecise when heard by algorithms. It was much easier, and more convenient to stand in front of a physical bookshelf, and pull out books at random, scanning the spines for unfamiliar names of authors. The authors in alphabetical order, not popped to the top of any Google search as if the most popular author is more important than every other author on the planet. Also, the randomness of physical bookstore browsing allowed me to discover new authors, like a bees buzzing among flowers. Again, my choices not directed by any mathematics or any preferential placement on a web-page.

Many young people do not seem to notice how everything they see is controlled, filtered, propagandized, and cleverly marketing by algorithms. The new young talents are only recognized when they become preferred destinations of the internet algorithms. That means most writers will never have more than a few hundred readers. The audience is not limited by the genius or attractiveness of the author's work, the audience is limited by the mechanics of the internet.

All forms of original new art get buried so deep, 30 pages deep in a Google search, where few people will have the patience to travel. Recognition and popularity rely on trendy gatekeepers, who are also so overwhelmed with content, they end up choosing to promote this or that work at random.

I say all this, knowing I have written some poems and stories equal to the work of many famous writers from the 20th Century, and here in the 21st Century there are few ways to get my work in front of the eyes of eager readers. Traditional book publishers are as lost in the new age of algorithms as anyone. They can spend millions of dollars on ad space, and push a few authors forward. Physical and e-books end up in public libraries, but much work is lost, never seen at all. Here we notice artistic quality is not the problem. *Distribution* of books and music, and many forms of art, has fallen apart under the sensory overload of the web.

I created my *Literary Broadsheets*, with the intention of printing 2000 to 4000 copies of each 20-page paper, a way to bring physical printed literature into people's hands. So far, that remains a future goal, as printing those quantities cost more money than I have. Also physical distribution remains problematic, as the pandemic continues, as weekly and monthly free newspapers are barely staying in business. Fewer people walk around and pickup free papers on street-corners.

The advantage of a poem printed on a piece of paper is its physical existence, more tangible, and easier to access than a digital poem. An unknown author has little chance of being found on the internet. One poem, printed in 3000 papers might reach 1000 people. And then the author is *known* to 1000 people.

ROSCOE FORTHRIGHT'S

LITERARY
BROADSHEET

Vol. 1   Issue 1   July 2021

ENTRY #4

I am not accustom to anger. Perhaps once a year I feel intense
anger, and it swirls into rage, as I have so little experience
with that emotion, I have less control over it than with my
feelings of love, or my feelings of tenderness. Usually anger
rises from a personal abuse, some person in my life taking
advantage of my generosity, over-stepping all lines of
courtesy or respect or loyalty, and blatantly lying to me or
stealing money from me, or both. Or intruding into my life
demanding I take on problems they created and make them
my own, and spend my money fixing those problems.
Mostly it s the lying and lack of personal loyalty, among
people I trust, people I have known for years, who decide they
can take my for every dime I have, as if I will not notice.

Fuck.   I look around and make the decision to remove those
people from my life. To give them no further benefit of doubt,
and no further kindness or generosity. I do not live to
shoulder the mistakes or failings of other people. Why do
they believe that is my purpose? I have never told them in
any way that is my purpose. They make it my purpose
through willful lack of respect for me. And that is the core of
my anger. Willful disrespect directed toward me and toward
my life, as if none of my previous, continual and long-
standing generosity matters at all.   Instant amnesia!

As if my kindness and support truly meant nothing at all. Obliviousness, or outright selfishness take over, and the girls, it is most often girls, take me for every dime they can get. This is more than *inconvenient*, when I find my debit card drained of funds, when I have bills to pay with that debit card and no other money available to pay those bills. Geez, Louise. That is a basic understanding and courtesy I thought every grown-up learns to live with... *NOT taking money* from other people, when they have been told clearly not to take money, because bills are coming due. Fuck me. Fuck me running.

It is worse when I have lived with the girl for several years, or and known her for a decade, and mostly trusted her in recent months and recent hours. It is simply insulting and impossible behavior. I cannot budget for my monthly and annual bills, AND leave room for random theft, coming unseen, without warning and draining the cash I had so carefully planned. The only solution to such a problem is to get rid of the thief, regardless of any previous and personal connection. Either that, or continue to live under the tyranny of random theft. No human female is worth that kind of trouble and anxiety. Many certainly appear to believe they are worth every penny they cajole, connive or steal. As if profuse apologies afterward, will keep the gravy train on the tracks, and ready to raid time and time again!

ENTRY #5

I will miss the cherubs, the beautiful young women who have been in my life over the past five years, now telling me with conviction, I must remove our videos from the internet to protect their relationships with husbands and boyfriends, and stating flatly, there will be no more sexual activity between us, though I may continue to video girl-girl sex action, because their husbands and boyfriends are OK with that. Well, fuck me. I have no interest at all in what their husband or boyfriends want, need or care about.... all that in none of my business and certainly not my responsibility and has never been my responsibility. And fuck me, I feel personally insulted and betrayed by the sweet cherubs who are always glad to take my money, and do whatever I asked them to to, and 99.9999% of the time they also had real, live orgasms in our videos. I was asking nothing of them they did not personally enjoy. And fuck me, now they announce the new rules, and somehow expect me to be OK with all that, and OK with the idea I need to live by the whims, vanities, fears and jealousies of their husbands and boyfriends, AND still pay each cherub a pile of cash to make more videos.

As with personal betrayals, and with outright theft of my money, the only useful response is: Eliminate these problems from my life. Get the cherubs to sprout wings and move on.

Get them far away, at such distance I will no longer speak to or have any interaction with, these particular, most lovely and most presumptuous group of cherubs. I will cause no threat to their loving relationships at home, because I will no longer be in their lives in any way. And about the videos.... some of them have already been copies and appear on websites far outside my reach and control. And the video on my own website can only be found if the husbands and boyfriends specifically go looking for them and know "Roscoe Forthright" by name. The math is easy. Less 30 people in the States of Washington and Oregon know Roscoe Forthright by name, and visit my website. Less than 3000 people in the entire U.S. know Roscoe Forthright by name. The percentage probability of one of those people having contact with a husband or a boyfriend is infinitesimally remote. As with the 4000 Roscoe Forthright viewers living in far distant countries. Also, *I own the videos* and the videos form the core of my website, and I do not like being told what to do with what I have bought and paid for, nor with my investment of time and money.

Frankly, my dear, I do not give a damn. What happens in your home is your business. And while I wish to cause no problems in their lives, it was in fact their personal choice to make videos with me, while knowing some future husband or boyfriend might not like it. To place that burden on me is a betrayal and disrespect for *the joy we honestly shared.*

ENTRY #6

Speaking of shared joy. I notice ex-relationships always include mild to severe forms of amnesia, as if hours, days, week and months of shared experience and shared joy, and shared orgasms never really happened. Yes. Let's all pretend what we both know happened, never really happened. Let's base our version of current loving-relationships on the precondition of mild to severe amnesia for everything which preceded the current relationship. What is the honest value of the love of husbands or boyfriends who perceive past events as threats, or hold the girls guilty of past naughtiness with other men. Fuck me. Do my cherubs want grown-up relationships, or Middle-School anxiety-ridden vanity-driven, jealousy-sparking relationships?

They speak with glowing words of adoration for their husbands and boyfriends: "I cannot live without him." "I will do nothing to hurt him or make him jealous." "I get wet just looking at him." Etc, etc, etc. All that is wonderful and pleasant, but if the man in question chooses to feel hurt or jealous over some sex scene in some past-tense video, there is nothing the little cherub can do about it. Any attempt to erase *all evidence* in the age-of-the-internet is an impossibility. So let them attempt the impossible if that makes them feel loyal. But I have no sense of loyalty to men I have never met, and never wish to meet. I own them nothing at all.

Oneness, in my mouth, in my vagina

by Beth Darmstadt

I love the feel and texture of your warm flesh
in my mouth, your soft cock growing full.

In my mouth you ache and quiver,
as my pussy splashes wet,
as close to God and Lord Jesus
as most people ever get,
our love-play more fun than
any devout and lovely prayer
ever written in any religion.

When our hearts open wide
ready to love and to be loved,
when are bodies are fully aroused,
when we sustain our ecstasy
long enough to pay attention,
long enough to learn from the event...

Oneness becomes possible.
Oneness in the sense of Buddhist Nirvana,
Islamic Oneness of God, available to us,
a Jewish personal covenant with God,
a Christian touching the Mind of God.
We take our religion one step further.

At the peak of orgasm,
In the sustained instant of time
when our minds and bodies vibrate,
so full of joy we can hardly stand it,
In the sustained instant of time,
when we are paying attention,
we can merge, become One
with the Eternal Oneness.

Try this for yourselves.
You need not take my word for it.
I rely on no Holy Books
written thousands of years ago.
I rely on personal experience,
and I am just telling you about it.
I am no evangelist going door to door.
I am no Vatican, ridiculously self-confident.

In our ecstatic moments
when our minds and spirit float
above the sexual pleasures,
we use our bodies like well-made boats,
Viking ships with all oars in the water,
to carry us places we can discover
in no other way, by no other means.
In other words, cocks and pussies
are fiery religious chariots,
more reliable than any rule book
collected from ancient languages,
with nothing we can touch and feel.

My body fully aroused,
my eyes sparkle, I bite my lip,
and I am certain all those stark
medical and scientific descriptions
of orgasms truly miss the point.
Like a Google algorithm attempting
to define God by searching databases.
It will never work. Computers
do not have orgasms, and will
never ever have orgasms.

I bite my lip as I watch your cock
full up, pointing toward God,
my fingertips move across, over
and around the mushroom head.
I make detailed maps with my tongue,
and press the tip into your small orifice.
This is what explorers do. Look around
and make accurate maps of the place.

I take the mushroom tight in my mouth.
I suck out your sacred ejaculate. Yes!
Yes! Yes! You come in my mouth
as I suck, as I squeeze your balls.
If this is not a religious experience
I have no idea why it feels so good,
as if God designed orgasms
for this specific holy purpose.

I do not stop with your ejaculation.
The lesson is not complete.
I spend time with semen on my tongue,
to notice the salty flavor and slickness,
and I swallow. I swallow your cream

because that is the only sensible
thing to do with sacred semen.
In fact, scientists say, semen is nutritious:
Fructose, Ascorbic acid, Zinc, Protein,
Calcium, Citric acid, Magnesium,
Vitamin B12, Vitamin C, Sodium,
Potassium, Lactic acid and Nitrogen.
Though never enough to live on.
My minimal daily requirement for orgasms
always larger than the supply of nutrients.
For spiritual purposes, those details do not matter.

I come and come and come
as you gush cream into my mouth!
I come and come and come
as you gush cream into my vagina!
(And my anus is also available
if you ever choose to travel there.)
Our fiery chariots, our Viking ships,
our bodies carry us over seas
uncharted by all the people
who stayed home mumbling
mantras or counting beads
and consulting venerable scholars
to explain obscure passages in Hebrew,
Arabic, Aramaic, Pâli or Sanskrit.

With first-hand experience of God,
like a Sufi whirling and singing,
beating drums and playing the ney,
like a Buddhist in eight states of trance,
Rumi and Hafez are much closer to us
than anything written by Martin Luther.

First-hand experience of God,
in the deepest core of each orgasm.
Now you are laughing, laughing,
thinking this nude young woman
is off her rocker, on thin ice
with no philosophic snowshoes,
nothing to hold her up, except
her own sweet ass, and those
wonderful, lovely breasts,
and oh, oh my God...
her pierced pubic folds
and her orgasmic vagina.
Truthfully, no philosophic snowshoes
are needed under such warm circumstances,
and why would anyone even bother to ask,
to ask nonsense questions, taking notes,

when God is obviously standing right here.

ENTRY #7

I am thinking about the tenuous relationship between any writer and their audience. The well-paid writers for television of film production, and a few speech writers have a guaranteed, captive audience. Listeners will hear whatever is thrown at them, and through pre-programmed formats and structures, those writers become skilled craftsmen, pouring specific and limited sets of ideas into tidy packages, suitable for framing, contained within well-established sets of rules.

Poets, novelists and spurious writers like myself, who may or may not earn one thin dime from their creations, move the art of language into new landscapes, often with ideas unpalatable to the current fads of social, economic, religious and political propaganda. The high-paid fiction writers and speech writers are often the ingenious creators of such propaganda, and their specific phrases getting repeated over and over in media broadcasts and public conversation, as if those phrases have some relationship to observable reality. Often, the slick propaganda has no connection at all to reality. The words attempt to invent a specific version of reality in the minds of the readers or listeners, statements pushing one to two small versions of truth, with specific goals and agendas. That is why those writers are the best paid of anyone. They *create* popular reality, and give people specific language to use.

The other writers push whatever version of truth seems to suit themselves, or their small groups of readers. On most online blogs the largest and most active audience *are other writers*, Readers wanting entertainment look..... God's only knows where. Our internet is so distracted and diverse, a reader can entertain themselves for years, reading, or listening to, short inconsequential sound-bytes on a wide array of subjects, with little art, and few long-term, accurate descriptions of human existence. Thoughtful expressions of fundamental problems with our civilization, or any specific aspect of our civilization, ... those well-thought, and well-articulated ideas are rarely, heard or read by millions of people, once or twice in every ten or twenty years, and often soon forgotten. As with current racial/social activists promoting hate, while ignoring provable facts, while ignoring most of what Martin Luther King, and much of what Malcolm X had to say about the reality of their time. The fundamental reality then, and the fundamental reality now is: Poverty fucks-up people's lives. Poverty shows no racial discrimination. All skin-colors are fucked when they live in poverty, with no opportunities and no good jobs. The tight control of economic opportunity, and an elite class, *hell-bent on Oligarchy*, causes most existent suffering. Racism is an invented problem, within the larger context of economic enslavement of tens of millions of people of all races, colors and creeds. The elite oligarchy are not racists. They hate everyone, and use everyone equally for self-profit.

Racism has become the political and social talking point, as if that was a real and urgent problem. The whole point of that national propaganda is to divert everyone's attention from the actual, *civilization-killing* problem of consolidation and control of all wealth by a tiny elite class of oligarchs. That is the problem the oligarchs wish to delete from public discourse. And they use the loud, righteous smoke-screen of racism, as an attempt to divert everyone's attention from large, growing and brutal *actual problems.*

When the large *civilization-killing* agendas are not included in public discourse, and not included in educational programs... what is left to talk about other than the propaganda? I had a shocking conversation with a grade school teacher, preparing to restart in-person class room education after almost two years of Covid. In Washington State, all teacher were are required to listen to and participate in, American Slavery training (critical race theory) that is, three days of mandatory propaganda having nothing to do with getting school up and running.
It is a Liberal agenda's mandated training, which allows lawmakers to tell the Liberal voters, *all is well,* and blacks will be treated fairly, with no racism in our schools. Blacks of course, are already treated fairly. The larger problem is paying teachers well enough so the good teachers do not quit. Of course, that is not on the list of propaganda talking points.

ENTRY #8

Today I created a 32-minute video, a goodbye to the young women I have loved over the past five years, the girls in my many Roscoe Forthright videos. Oh, I did truly enjoy each one, and did my best to please them, and make their lives easier, most often with cash!! Seven young beautiful women. The eighth young woman still lives in my house, and has given me no reason to expel her from my life.

The others, each gave me specific, tangible and unsolvable reasons. Only one left in anger. The others decided their husbands and boyfriends were more relevant in their lives than myself. And that was absolutely accurate in almost every way.   Not that my love nor generosity were lacking. It is my inability to spend time and energy on long-term relationships, while remaining an active and busy composer. This is my choice, partly from an innate belief no love relationship with a woman would remain satisfactory over the next twenty years of my life, that is, the last two decades of my life. My artistic ambitions are far more powerful than any romantic ambition. That is the construct of my psyche.

So each girl maybe a correct choice. I call my film: "Collection of Temporary Joys."

ENTRY #9

I am never ready for good friends to die. Knowing several
of my good friends are over 70, and some over 80, does not
make it easier, or more expected. Yes. I know any of these
fellows can croak at any moment. Over 70 life is tenuous,
death from any number of reasons, even without cause more
dramatic than old age. The skin we walk in is finite. The
good people inside are infinite.

Karl's death, occurring in the same week as my decision to
remove myself from the lives of my lovers, gives me more
reason than ever to focus on the most important actions, and
the most important ideas of each day. To keep short-term
distractions to a minimum, pay close attention to my work, to
compose music, and more music. To write the most precise
and worthwhile literature I can invent. To observe. To
comment. To form opinions about cause and effect. To form
religious opinions without any frame of reference other than
my personal experience. That is, I do not rely on ancient
back-stories, and accumulated cosmic explanations of our
major and minor religions. God, Oneness, Divine Grace,
Divine Influence, all those states of being are to be
experienced. The ancient stories were often attempts to
explain such personal spiritual experiences.

My life, my connection to Oneness is no less personal in the 21st Century than monks with dirty feet 2500 years ago. Careful observation of Reality, and specifically Spiritual Reality, still yields results. The back-stories are no more relevant than my own spiritual experiences.

In this way, my life becomes more urgent, with less time to waste on collections of temporary joy. Nothing wrong with temporary joy, except it distracts me from the main event, that spiritual event which is my daily existence. Delightful temporary joys distract my from the exploration and understanding of the main event. Composing music is a direct spiritual experience. At least, it is in my way of life. It demands my full attention to compose worthwhile music. It demands a vision which reaches further than current trends of artistic fashion, and beyond the reach of both music theory and music critics. A music critics job is to sell tickets. If he is just making witted commentary and selling no tickets, he is an objective failure. Musician and composers need paying work, and the only job of the music critic is get a paying audience into the seats.

The writing above is a concise example of my stream-of-consciousness writing, blending spiritual awareness with the very practical concerns of musicians making money, keeping the lights turned on in symphony halls, where violinists, violists, cellists, clarinet and french horn players make a living, from decent paying jobs in professional orchestras. Having met the orchestral players in Lviv, and having a concern for their future works, and the future work of all talented and well-trained musicians. I believe music critics should keep their mouths shut unless they have some tickets to sell.

These are the urgent concerns: The creation of art, the promotion of my best art, the recording of my best art, and all the practical daily choices which allow for the creation of art. Each orchestral work I compose, may provide a stage-full of musicians paying work, next year, the year after, ten and twenty years from now. I notice the old repertoire, the remarkable masterworks of previous centuries, will not keep orchestra in business. New and younger audiences require contemporary works as well crafted as the old repertoire, and more relevant to our own place and time. Give me a "C" !!

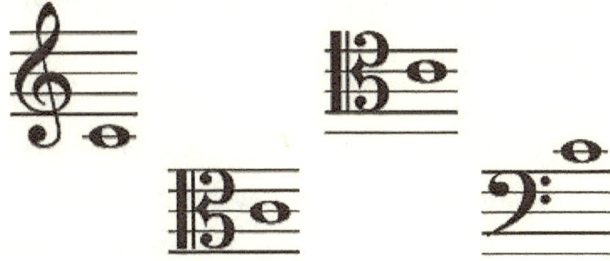

ENTRY #10

I compose music for the joy of it. I know some people
compose music for many other reasons. Some Hollywood
compose for large piles of cash, and care more about the new
additions to their homes, and their yacht-club memberships
than they do about the act of composing music, and the
spiritual experience of composing and listening to music.
Few works of the past century contain spiritual joy, which is
obvious in older works, and essential to the creation of those
old masterpieces. Most living composers write few
masterpieces, or none at all. We are not encouraged to do so
by the civilization we live in. The creators of Google and
global marketing find little value in the form of art, known as
classical music. Technologies and psychological manipulation
appear to be more important to their daily lives than spiritual
experiences, and specifically more important than the joyful
spiritual importance of art, art of all kinds, not only classical
music. Money seems to win out over spiritual joy on most
days, if we judge corporate and government leaders by their
public statements and daily behavior.

Most days, I honestly do not care what any corporate or
government leader has to say. As they live in a separate
universe from my universe; our lives barely intersect at all.
They are noticeable only in negative impacts. Like asteroids.

As with Covid-mask mandates making groceries more difficult to buy, destroying the economy, causing some restaurants, and other businesses in my small community to close, and never reopen. I can avoid such negative impacts no more than I can avoid asteroids. The logic and trajectory of corporate and government leaders contains no vector of predicable pattern, except as with asteroids, they push their way into our air, and destroy our land and lives without one trace of sentimentality or conscience.

Am I too harsh in my judgment of men and women I have never met, and will never meet? I do not think so. I have met our current Governor of Washington State, the man personally responsible for the destruction of local economies and fear-mongering in the lives of millions of people. Before he was Governor, sitting outside a movie theater on Bainbridge Island, close to his money-man (the entire reason for his existence as a political leader.) At the time, Jay Inslee talked like a reasonable and rational human being. Only a few years later, he behaved as he was told to behave, a complete stooge of Democratic Party agendas. The rational idea: *Covid is not a local or national disaster,* did not cross his mind at all. He pushed forward, and continues to push forward the brutal nonsenses, as he is told to do. Who does he care about? Who does the Democratic Party care about? It 's not me. Not the owners of closed businesses. Who?

I lose all respect for powerful people when they no longer make a reasonable effort to behave in rational ways. As with the leaders of Boeing, pretending they did not personally make decisions which caused planes to fall out of the sky and kill 346 people. The Boeing engineers told the executives the planes were not ready to sell. And the engineers were told to shut up, and not talk about that anymore.

As a rational person and as a composer of music I see very little connection between myself and people who live in the large world of big money and politics, as if I am a stranger visiting their planet, or they are marauding space-pirates attacking my planet, whenever they feel like it, for no good reason at all. I notice these particular bands of pirates remain self-righteous, and hold a moral high ground in their own perception of themselves. And that makes them entirely impossible to communicate with in any known language. The pirates are certain their rape, pillage, murder, scorched and salted earth are the best solutions to social and economic problems. Mostly, men like Jay Inslee do what they are told, and the only objective of their pirate leadership is control over the lives of other people for the purpose of making piles of cash, for themselves and their cheerless group of oligarchs. What appalls me most is their pathetic lack of creative imagination. That is even more disgusting than their lack of moral conscience.

ENTRY #11

We deserve better than this. The good, moral citizens of the United States deserve Statesmen, not demented, senile, elitist clowns. The fact remains, the majority of citizens in the U.S. work hard and have a collective morality, a sense of goodness and generosity and tolerance for their fellow citizens. We do not here much about that fact on the Evening News. We are barraged nightly with nonsense, usually Liberal Democratic agenda nonsense, about this or that under-served and down-trodden minor, the Blacks, the LGBTQs, whoever is on the list this week. We are, for two years, barraged with Covid bullshit nonsense, and yesterday the Demented President is pushing even more for vaccinations for tens of millions of citizen. Absolute and complete nonsense, with no basis in physical reality. The only reality is clown-leaders continuing to push around 330 to 360 million people in the U.S., because they can. For no other reason. Making money from Covid paranoia is another reason, but not the main motivation. The ruling oligarchs want to see how far they can push the sheep-like people, how many months they can extent the grotesque fraud of Covid, before millions of citizen will deliberately and willful refuse to comply with Federal and State mandates and regulations. The ruling elite want to know the breaking-point, for future reference. The ruling elite has ambitions far larger the scaring us with Covid.

For future control and exploitation of U.S. citizens, the elite needs to know which forms of propaganda and coercion deliver the best results. That is, getting the largest number of people to do what they are told for the longest duration.

I offer the above as a possible explanation for the bizarre behavior of most world leaders over the past two years. The elites are testing the waters, seeing which populations can be pushed hard, and for how long. My assessment may or may not be accurate. I do believe the smart people who tell the clown-leaders what to do and say have specific goals. The actual leaders of the world, the people whose names we barely hear, the leader who stay in the shadows, running the clowns, sending in more clowns.... those smart oligarchs are not playing games with all of us. They truly wish to know what is required for absolute control, and absolute theft of all available wealth and property. The end goal is maximum acquisition of all valuable assets, within the span of their lifetimes, that is, with the span of forty to fifty years. The end goal is the creation of an cohesive band of billionaires. We currently have 614 billionaires in the U.S. The elites want to grow slightly, to include enough billionaires, perhaps as many as 2000 people, to consolidate complete control over all wealth, to decimate the middle-class and make debt slaves of them, and continue to have the low class for serfs, and fodder for the machines, bodies required to make more money.

ENTRY #12

My young lovers are exquisite and beautiful. They create
spiritual experiences, as they are naked with wet vaginae, as
they sock my soft or erect cock. Stella and Codie have never
held my flesh in their mouths, and probability never will.
Codie has jacked me; Stella has not. I have licked the aroused
vaginae of Virginia, Eva, Kim, Bea and Olivia. Virginia Eva,
Kim, Codie, Stella, Bea, Olivia and Anna have had orgasms
with me close by. Other with a video camera documenting the
events. After a few years, none of those details matter. What
remains relevant are the instances of shared love. Not all these
women have generous capacity in that regard, Three or four
remain constant in my life, those women create variety, joy,
tenderness and large amounts of love. In my life, for me, the
shared orgasms were a starting-point for ongoing and useful
form of love, love between grown-ups, inspiring love,
friendship and the joy of love, which was and is separate from
their romance ambitions with their own boyfriends and
husbands. Friendship is easier without the burden of romantic
expectations.

Do not misunderstand, I love to gush semen for each of these
girls, and I would enjoy having closer relations with a few.
Being 30 to 40 years older, romance has little chance to
remain solid. A snowball's chance in Hell.

I have no illusions about what our relationships are, and what they are not. They are relationships caused, and perpetuated by a flow of cash from my wallet into their purses. And I have no problem with that. I enjoy supporting the lives of each lively young woman. Some more than others. I take what I can get, and am happy with the situation. When I cannot hold Codie's breasts in my hands, and suck her eager aroused nipples, I hold Eva's breasts. When I cannot lick Eva's vagina, I lick Kim's vagina. When I cannot lick Kim's vagina, I enjoy Virginia sucking me, and sucking me some more.

Other girls come and come, and go and go. Over four or five years some exit my life, never to return. Being a practical man, I expect most all of them will exit within the next ten years. I hold no fantasies about long-term, lifetime lovers. Human rarely manage that. We are far more often distracted, frivolous, shallow, almost innately superficial in our relations with each other. Long-term grown-up relationships require effort and patience, over months, years and decades. Far longer than the attention-span of most people. Many existing long-term relationships remain from habit, more than from daily, ecstatic mutual joy. Ask any person who has been marry for twenty to forty years. The accomplishment is more psychological endurance than romantic enthusiasm.

ENTRY #13

When a former lover gets married, especially a young lover,
no thoughtful person can keep their mind quiet nor their
mouth shut.   This is what I told Codie:

"I created an 8-min tribute to you and me. NOBODY gets to
see this video, except you and me. I will post it nowhere, ever.
I send it because, you were there, and you were happy... and
I love you like a daughter and like a past lover. These are
really wonderful and important memories for me. There have
been only two or three people in my 64-year life who have
made me as happy as you. Eva is one of them. Think about
that for a minute. I lived close to 60 years *without* my current
joyful friendships and sexual happiness. All the other women
(*50 years of women*) came and went, leaving no lasting
impression at all, and no lasting joy at all.

I am here for you now, *like a good Daddy,* in the background,
staying out of the way, and giving you some back-up security,
someone to talk to, and get money from if you need it."

50 years of women is a lot of unimportant women, women
who had no interest in me, or honest loving girls who did not
get me excite at all, and some hot girls with minor interest in
me, but nothing to extend further than a year or two.

ENTRY #14

Classical music lovers might wonder what Sibelius or Bartok
or Brahms or Mozart felt about their work, and what they felt
during the composition of their work. Most major composers
were not specifically articulate about either subject. Many
minor composers, as in the 20th Century spoke and wrote for
days about their work!! Most of these men where university
professors, and therefore required to talk about composition,
and much of what they say is of use to no one at all. The vast
intellectual theories amount to gossip when compared to the
actual experience of composing a worthwhile piece of music,
specifically a piece other humans enjoy. Much of the music
composition of the 20th Century were admired only by the
composers and their fellow college and university professors.
The general concert-goer audience was left dismayed, and
even snubbed, as being unsophisticated and plebeian in their
musical tastes. The plebs however, most often paid the bills,
supporting the local symphony orchestras, and paying the
salaries of the college and university professors when sending
children to music schools. The plebs got entirely tired of this
situation, and in many places ceased to support contemporary
music in anyway in the United States. Some countries in
Europe have slightly more tolerant audiences, and continue
to listen and support contemporary music. Generally, only a
handful of composers come to public attention.

The U.S. "art grants" become the place for contemporary music and the other arts, and this was, and still is problematic. The government grants are required to go to "under-served" Native Americans, Blacks, Gays or whatever other subset of humanity is currently popular as a Liberal Agenda talking point. In other words, arts grant are most often political or social agendas having little or nothing to do with the quality or long-term value of the art being produced. Other course, no one wants to says this truth bluntly. That is what happens when the paying audience has no honest interest in the art or music being produced. The social and political agendas, and committee meetings determine which artist are supported. The receiving audience has no say in the matter at all. And the audience probably prefers it that way. Having decided 10, 20 and 30 years ago, all contemporary is inferior to the great art of past centuries, and not even worth bothering with.

After all this, now twenty years into the 21st Century, most living art is ignored, or lost in the distraction and noise of the Internet. Specific artists are pushed into public spotlights, now and then, usually the result of expensive marketing of one sort or another, and many talents remain unknown, even to sincere Classical music lovers, who would indeed enjoy the music of these unknown composers, if they were given an opportunity to hear the music. Even when recording are available, they remain obscure on small record labels.

Most programming of contemporary works remains tightly controlled by social or political agendas, or the amount of money spent by the composer, or the deep-pocket benefactors of this or that composer. It is for this reason, we have no Sibelius, Bartok, Mozart or Brahms living in the U.S. today, and known, and enjoyed by thousands of people. They symphony orchestra business-model truly does not allow such talents to come to the attention of large audiences. Likewise, and especially so with mass media, which acts as if classical music, poets and painters of provable genius do not exist at all, in any corner of our planet. Mass media pushes forward artists in the same manner as government arts grants, for reasons having nothing at all to do with the quality of the art or the audience for the art.

After all this, if some Classical music lover still wished to know what active, living orchestral composers think about, and feel about the music they create-- I am glad to say what I know. The film composers are the orchestral composers heard by more people than the audience of all other living classical composing combined. The film composers are a small subset of living composers, and their work is limited in value, specifically because the music is composed as support to the larger art-form of film, supporting whatever story is being told. The music is rarely structured to stand on its own as a satisfying concert work. Bluntly, the music is superficial.

And has little opportunity to be anything other than
superficial, being constrained in both content and form.
There are brilliant moments in the best films scores, but those
moments are not sustained for twenty or thirty minutes as in a
symphony by Sibelius, Brahms, Haydn and other past genius
composers. A few living genius composer exist and work
every day, completely overshadowed by the work of film
composers, as the film composers are the only ones mentioned
in mass media. With rare exceptions, living composers
generally have only regional recognition in their own town,
or in whatever town their music is most performed.

Being a living composer, I can say I do not like this situation at
all. The only benefit to being completely unknown is: No one
pesters me, and my names is never mentioned in the tabloids.
I can be as perverse and roguish as I want to be, and truly no
one knows or cares. Opportunities for public performance
range of extremely rare to non-existent. There is no money
in it. Most living composer compose because because they
have a personal need to do so. A need as serious as waking up
and eating breakfast. As serious as earning money to pay rent
and buy groceries. While most composer have small or non-
existent audiences, the composer still know when they have
created worthwhile music, and enjoys their creations, with no
applause from anyone. They satisfy their innate artistic needs
as best they can under quiet and obscure circumstances.

When a man speaks words of truth he
speaks words of greatness:
Know the nature of truth.

When a man knows Oneness, he can
speak truth. One who knows
nothing about Oneness, cannot speak
truth:
Know the nature of knowledge.

When a man thinks then he can know.
He who does not think
does not know: Know the nature of
thought.

When a man has faith then he thinks.
He who has know faith
does not think: Know the nature of
faith.

Where there is progress one sees and has
faith. Where there is no progress there is
no faith: Know the nature of progress.

Where there is creation there is progress.
Where there is no creation there is no
progress: Know the nature of creation.

Where there is joy there is creation.
Where there is no joy
there is no creation: Know the nature of
joy.

Where there is the Infinite there is joy.
There is no joy in the finite.
Only in the Infinite there is joy: Know
the nature of the Infinite.

Where nothing else is seen, or heard, or
known there is the Infinite.
Where something else is seen, or heard,
or known there is the finite.
The Infinite is immortal; but the finite is
mortal.

Where does the Infinite rest? On his
own greatness, or not even
on his own greatness.

In this world they call greatness the
possession of cattle and horses,
elephants and gold, servants and wives,
lands and houses. But I do not call this
greatness, for here one thing depends
upon another.

But the Infinite is above and below,
North and South and East and West.
I am the whole universe.

I am above and below, North and South
and East and West.
Atman is the whole universe.

He who sees, knows, and understands
this, who finds in Atman, the Spirit,
his love and his pleasure and his union
and his joy,
becomes the Master of himself. His
freedom is infinite.

But those who do not see this become
servants of other masters
in the worlds that pass away, and attain
no liberation.

Chandogya Upanishad no. 7, verses 16 to 25.

The image below is from a *Chandogya Upanishad* manuscript.
It is the second oldest known Upanishads, dated to between
900 to 600 BCE (pre-Buddhist era.)

FREEMASONRY

If we are talking about mysterious and wonderful spiritual ideas, let us consider Freemasonry. Young men who visit Masonic Lodges quickly discover, there are old men who have interesting things to say, even before the old gentlemen have ingested small or large quantities of distilled alcohol. Young men who do not have older men to hang out with, to have conversations with, truly miss out on valuable pieces of information, information which cannot be received in any other way. Older men, from the simple act of being alive forty to sixty years longer than oneself, hold worldviews much different than most young people. Young people who form worldviews, only by talking with other young people are not likely to get anywhere close to a complete picture of reality.

Some social organizations, and their philosophical ideas have lasted more than 300 or 400 years for good reasons. The organizations and ideas have valuable qualities, which translate well, and remain meaningful across several generations, across economic, political and religious separateness. One rule held firmly in most Masonic Lodge is: No discussion of religion or politics within the Lodge-Room, as those topics tend to divide people rather than unite people. Brotherly Love and Friendship can be strained under the influence of strongly opposed opinions.

Level contentious discussion for outside the Lodge, or during dinner. Bring no contentious behavior into the Lodge-Room.

The Masonic attitude is a practical application of Oneness. We are all Brothers. Let us for an hour or so, set aside our differences and act like Brothers. Some notable examples of this are British and American soldiers attending Lodge together during the Revolutionary War. And going back to the battlefield the following day. During the Revolutionary War, there were two occasions where warrants, jewels, tools and furniture from a British military Lodge were captured by American forces, and records show that under a flag of truce and a procession of honor guards, these items were properly returned. It is clear Freemasonry held firm and supported both Colonial and British brethren. Such Masonic behavior occurred during the U.S. Civil War, and several other wars. Masons recognizing other Masons, and fulfilling their duty to each other as human beings, as well as fulfilling their duty as soldiers.

The Obligation of the Entered Apprentice Degree,
the First Degree of Freemasonry:

I, Roscoe Forthright, of my own free will and accord, in the
presence of Almighty God and this right Worshipful Lodge of
ancient free and accepted Masons on the first degree of
Masonry, erected to Him and dedicated to the holy Saints
John, do hereby and hereon solemnly and sincerely promise
and swear that I will always heal, ever conceal, and never
reveal any of the secret arts, parts, or points of the mysteries
of Freemasonry which have been, may now, or shall at any
future time be communicated to me, or in anyway come to my
knowledge to any person, except it be in a just and legally
constituted lodge, or to a known brother Mason. Nor to him
or them til by strict trial, due examination or legal Masonic
information I shall have found him or them as Justly entitled
to the same.

I furthermore solemnly swear that I will not write, indite, cut,
carve, print, paint, stamp, stain, mark or engrave the same on
anything movable or immovable under the canopy of heaven
and will make no letter, figure, character, or cypher legible or
intelligible to myself or any other person whereby the secrets
of free Masonry maybe unlawfully obtained. All which I
solemnly and sincerely promise and swear with a fixed and
steady purpose of mind to keep and perform without

hesitation, mental reservation or secret evasion of mind, binding myself under the no less penalty than that of having my throat cut from ear to ear, my tongue torn out by its roots and buried in the rough sands of the sea, a cable-tows length from shore where the tide ebbs and flows twice in twenty-four hours, so help me, God, and keep me steadfast in this my Entered Apprentices solemn obligation.

Commentary:

All Freemasons, over the past three hundred years have solemnly sworn this obligation, or words very close to it, among their Brothers within a tiled Lodge of Freemasons. They state clearly and without hesitation their loyalty to each other, including the guarding of secret knowledge imparted to them. The colorful language was carefully written to create an emotional response, and be memorable, even shocking on first hearing. Most candidates for the Degrees of Freemasonry have not seen nor heard this Obligation until the moment they are in Lodge Ritual, surrounded by Brothers. The words spoken to them, and the candidate repeating the Obligation as he swear to upon each portion of it.

The seriousness of intention is the primary function of the First Degree. This is for grown-ups. Obligations between Brothers. The First Bond of Brotherhood.

The Obligation of the Fellowcraft Degree,
the Second Degree of Freemasonry.

I, Brother Roscoe Forthright, of my own free will and accord,
in the presence of Almighty God and this Worshipful Lodge of
Ancient Free & Accepted Masons on the second degree of
Masonry erected to Him and dedicated to the Holy Saints John
do here on solemnly swear, that I will always hele, ever
conceal and never reveal any of the secrets of the Fellow Craft
degree that have been, may be now, or at any future time
communicated to me or in any way come to my knowledge to
any person, except it be in a regular lodge on the second
degree of Masonry or to a known Brother Fellow Craft, nor
unto him or them until by strict trial, due examination or
lawful Masonic information I shall have found him or them as
justly entitled to the same as I am about to be.

I furthermore solemnly swear that I will due obedience pay to
the officers of this or any other Lodge in all their lawful
Masonic workings. I furthermore solemnly swear that I will
due answer make to all signs and summonses sent to and
received by me by a Fellow Craft lodge if within the length of
my cable-tow. I furthermore solemnly swear that I will aid
and assist all distressed Brother Fellow Craft they applying to
me as such and I finding them worthy, so far as their necessity
may require and my ability to perform will admit.

I furthermore solemnly swear that I will not cheat, wrong or defraud a Brother Fellow Craft, nor supplant him in any of his laudable undertakings, knowing him to be such.

To all this I solemnly swear with a fixed and steady purpose, to keep and perform without hesitation, mental reservation or secret evasion of mind, binding myself under no less penalty than that of having my breast torn open, my heart taken thence and exposed to the vultures of the air as a prey, should I violate this, my Fellow Craft solemn obligation, so help me God and keep me steadfast.

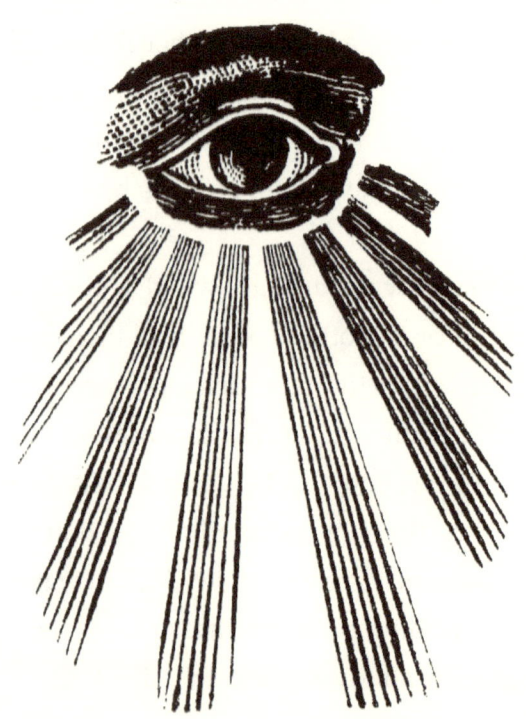

The Obligation of the Master Mason Degree,
the Third Degree of Freemasonry:

I, Roscoe Forthright, of my own free will and accord, in the presence of Almighty God and this Worshipful Master Mason's Lodge, erected to Him and dedicated to the Holy Saints John, due hereon most solemnly swear, that I will always hale, ever conceal and never reveal any of the secrets of the Master Mason's degree that have been, may be now, or at any future time communicated to me or in any way come to my knowledge to any person except it be in a legally constituted Master Mason's Lodge or to a known Brother Master Mason, nor unto him or them until by strict trial, due examination, or lawful Masonic information I shall have found him or them as justly entitled to the same as I am about to be.

I furthermore solemnly swear that I will stand to and abide by the laws, rules and regulations of this or any other Master Mason's Lodge of which I may be a member, and will maintain and support the laws, rules and edicts of the Grand Lodge under which the same may be holding, so far as they may come to my knowledge.

I further more solemnly swear that I will due answer make to all signs and summonses sent to and received by me from a Master Mason's Lodge if within the length of my cabletow.

I furthermore solemnly swear that I will aid and assist all distressed brother Master Masons, their widows and orphans, they making application to me as such and I finding them worthy, so far as I can without injury to myself or family. I furthermore solemnly swear that I will keep the secrets of a worthy brother Master Mason when communicated to and received by me as such, murder and treason excepted and these at my election.

I furthermore solemnly swear that I not cheat, wrong or defraud a brother Master Mason, nor speak evil of his good name or that of his family, nor permit it to be done by another if within my power to prevent, knowing him or them to be such.

I furthermore solemnly swear that I will not strike or otherwise offer personal violence to a brother Master Mason except it be in the necessary defense of my person, property or family, knowing him to be such.

I furthermore solemnly swear that I will not have illegal carnal communication with a brother Master Mason's wife, daughter, sister or mother nor permit it to be done by another if within my power to prevent, knowing them to be such.

I furthermore solemnly swear that I will not be at the initiating, passing or raising of an old man in dotage, a young man in nonage, a woman, an atheist or a fool, nor will I sit in a clandestine lodge or converse upon the secrets of Masonry with a clandestinely made Mason nor with one suspended or expelled while under such sentence, knowing him or them to be such.

I furthermore solemnly swear that I will not communicate the secret word of a Master Mason in any other way or manner than that in which I shall receive it.

To all this I most solemnly swear with a fixed and steady purpose to keep and perform without hesitation, mental reservation or secret evasion of mind, binding myself under no less penalty than that that of having my body severed in twain, my bowels taken thence, burned to ashes and scattered to the four winds of Heaven that there might remain no more remembrance among men or Masons of so vile a wretch as I should be to violate this, my Master Mason's most solemn obligation, so help me God and keep me steadfast.

Commentary:

The Fellowcraft and Mason Mason Degrees further strengthen the bond of trust and responsibility between Brothers. It is no wonder at all, Brothers who swear these Obligations feel united, even on opposing sides in battle. The Degree Rituals, symbols and obligations serve as a common ground, a philosophic understanding and acceptance between men, regardless of circumstance,political situations, economic differences, across the borders of many nations. *All Men Are Brothers* is the fundamental spiritual belief of Freemasonry, a belief very close to my understanding and my experience of Oneness.

In many places a further prayer is added, the Closing Prayer of many Lodges:

Brethren, you are now about to quit this sacred retreat of friendship and virtue, to mix again with the world. Amidst its concerns and employments, forget not the duties you have heard so frequently inculcated and forcibly recommended in this Lodge. Be diligent, prudent, temperate, and discreet.

Remember that, at this Altar, you have promised to befriend and relieve every Brother who shall need your assistance.

Remember also, that you have promised to remind him, in the most tender manner, of his failings, and aid his reformation; to remind him the the most friendly manner of his faults, and aid in his reformation of character. Let the world observe how Masons love one another.

These generous principles are to extend further. Every human being has a claim upon your kind offices. Do good unto all. Recommend it more especially to the household of the faithful. By diligence in the duties of your respective callings ; by liberal benevolence and diffusive charity; by constancy and fidelity in your friendships, discover the beneficial and happy effects of this ancient and honorable institution. Let it not be supposed that you have labored in vain, and spent your strength for naught; for your work is with the Lord and your recompense with your God. Finally, Brethren, be ye all of one mind; live in peace, and may the God of love and peace delight to dwell with and bless you!

ENTRY #16

Before we get whisked-off to spiritual planes and etheric
realms, let us return to the very human joys of physical life,
and the joys of the Elements: Air, Water, Earth, Fire.

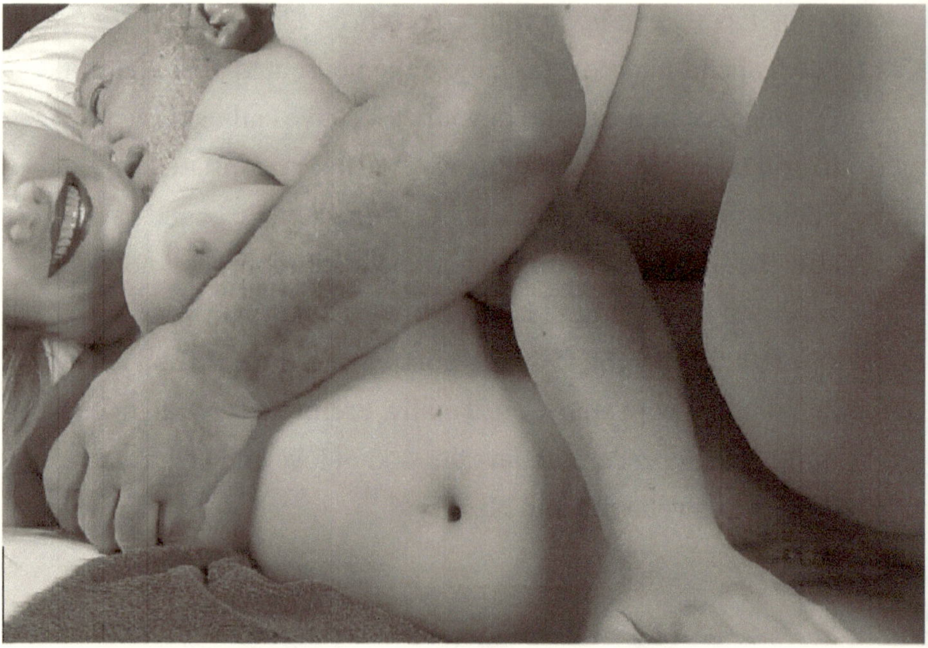

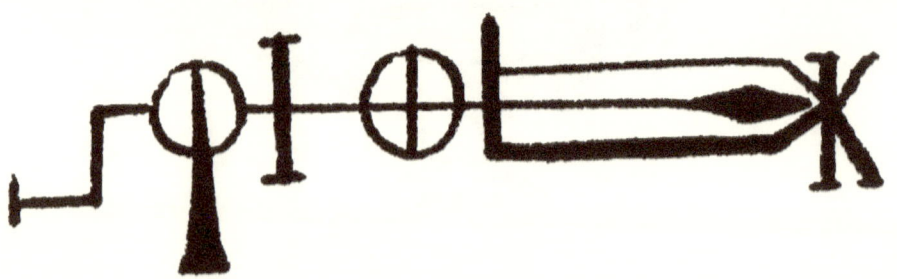

A Decent Wetness, Like Water

for Stella, the boat-girl

I cannot live away from Water.

My breasts float better in Water.

In Air they swing joyfully free,

refreshed cool air contracts my nipples.

But, Air remains insubstantial, blown

too fast, or tepid like a flaccid lover.

I prefer Earth, a solid firm place

to support my fanny, to place my feet firmly

when the boy on top pounds

and pounds and pounds. Oh! Even better,

cushioned with moss or cedar boughs,

when the girl kneels over my face

when I lick her folds, as she bounces

and comes, comes, comes!

Through all seasons essential, Fire,

for cooking and warmth, with or without

boy-friends or girl-friends, beautiful to watch.

I see flames. I see embers.

I see dead cold ashes.

As lovers come and come,

and go and go. Restless as Fire.

Of all the Primal Elements

I desire Water. I return to Water

again and again, always satisfied.

Its wetness much like my own,

a decent, reliable wetness:

rain, lakes, rivers and oceans,

with no extraneous demands,

an honest, intimate wetness:

steam, waterfalls, hot springs,

moist kisses and tears, even snow

I welcome with joy as quick

as crackling ice in my Mojito!

I am closest to you,

more ready than ever,

when I am in Water.

ROSCOE FORTHRIGHT'S

LITERARY
BROADSHEET

Vol. 1 Issue 1   July 2021

ENTRY #17

Balance remains essential in all things, for any person who wishes to have sustained joy, calmness and feelings of honest satisfaction. Some people are OK with sporadic bursts of joy, calmness and satisfaction, and make no deliberate plans to bring those moments into their lives. I am not one of those people. I know there are deliberate actions, and deliberate patterns of thought and behavior which lead to long-term positive results.

For example: A heterosexual male person who overwhelms their mind with spiritual learning, pursues purity and celibacy, and never boinks a pretty girl or two, misses out on essential facts and essential joys of human existence. Such people often become self-righteous and consider their lives morally super to lusty boys and girls who boink on numerous occasions. Various priesthoods, wish the world to believe they have an upper-hand in the possession of Divine Truth. As if Divine Truth is not available to uninitiated, millions of people, without the paid-for assistance of *Holy Gatekeepers*. That is nonsense for the purpose of making money, and always has been nonsense. Any All-Powerful, All-Knowing God, or Eternal Oneness, has the good sense not to make Themselves obscure, unknown, impossible to touch, impossible to enjoy.

An All-Mighty Deity, or Oneness, *reliant on* well-paid Gatekeepers appears to be the underlying assumption of some major religions. The Truth is: Any Eternal Being with their weight in Salt will not need human Gatekeepers, making money on Their Behalf, to bring the mass of humanity into Celestial Realms. Alert people, who are paying attention to what goes in around them, and paying attention to Nature, and Her methods of operation, will often lead themselves to spiritual experiences, without the prompting or tithing of expensive religions, nor supporting their expensive real estate.

It remains true, some reading and thoughtfulness, and good advice from honest and wise Elders can make a spiritual path less rocky, and help a person avoid the charlatans, con-men and thieves. Charlatans, con-men and thieves are as busy and numerous in religion, as they are in business, politics and many other areas of human endeavor. Money is far too attractive a goal for many people. The honest teachers will teach you for free, or for very little- a bowl of rice, a few dollars for groceries. Honest teachers of any religion, will not be raiding your wallet on every occasion for every possible reason. Temples are grand, beautiful, peaceful, and often sacred, but *truly unnecessary* for mature spiritual minds.

Deliberate actions and deliberate patterns of thought and behavior do more for a person than any priest or temple.

ENTRY #18   FRINGE LITERATURE

As a further education in Reality, let us discuss the physical existence of this book. You hold this *in your hands*, as it currently exists nowhere online as an e-book or pdf. As recently as five years ago, a book like this would not be printed and made available on Amazon, Barnes & Noble and other easily found online retail shops. Before now, a sick combination of censorship rules, and *political-correctness* rules would prevent mass-distribution of any book insulting all major religions, and talking extensively on the subject of boinking beautiful young women, while offering nude images of specific women the author has boinked. Even now, these things remain problematic, but the book exists, and it is held in your hands, because you heard of it somewhere, and acquired a copy.

Big, authorized, *legal-suit minded* book publishers will never publish a book like this one. Small presses in the 1970s and 1980s published such books, but those forms of publishing are long gone, put out of business almost completely by the internet. The demise of most physical books stores has made distribution of fringe literature almost non-existent. You hold in your hands, a re-birth of fringe literature. We will see how long this reincarnation lasts, before the corporate *authorized publishers* find a way to shut it down.

If lulu.com gets destroyed by some form of corporate or government lawsuits, making future publication and distribution impossible, fringe literature again, will cease to exist. People may write fringe literature, but few readers will ever see it, or even hear about it. For now, I get to say whatever I damn well please, and show erotic images to anyone who has interest in my ideas and my girls.

As if September 2021, here is what a Bing search of Roscoe Forthright looks like:

Literary Broadsheets

*https://www.lulu.com/en/us/shop/**roscoe-forthright**/...*

Jul 27, 2021· **Roscoe Forthright** now lives on AmberRiverwood.com ~ I notice current attempts to scrub-clean the internet, and scrub-clean public discourse, the attempt to be sensitive to the emotional triggers of other people, to censor our language, to censor our ideas, so no one will be offended, to use the correct pronouns when speaking to people who truly dress funny, and say they are sexually …

The Sacred Followers of Roscoe Forthright

*https://www.lulu.com/en/us/shop/**roscoe-forthright**/...*

Roscoe Forthright has brought those teachings into the 21st Century, and made the rituals relevant to modern spiritual seekers. Soon after his first publications, The Sacred Followers of **Roscoe Forthright** was established as a modern sex ritual cult, with physical Lodges in 57 cities in the U.S. and Canada, and 15 addition international Lodges.

Oneness by Roscoe Forthright, Hardcover | Barnes & Noble®

*https://www.barnesandnoble.com/w/oneness-**roscoe-forthright**/1139713801*

Jun 16, 2021· After four years online, **Roscoe Forthright** provides both fans and Followers a full explanation of his philosophy. He includes a complete view of his revelations about Oneness, and details on the influence of Buddhist, Hindu, Sufi and Taoist traditions...

Amazon.com lists two Roscoe Forthright books:

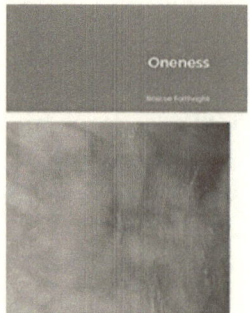

Oneness
by Roscoe Forthright | Jun 16, 2021

Hardcover

Out of Print--Limited Availability.

Literary Broadsheets
by Roscoe Forthright | Jul 27, 2021

Paperback

$22⁰⁰

✓prime Get it as soon as **Sun, Sep 19**

FREE Shipping on orders over $25 shipped by Amazon

In a Bing search, some of our x-rated videos appear, many do not. I expect all the x-rated videos will be removed within six to eight months, as the on-going *cleaning-scrubbing* of internet search engines continues to limit what people get to learn about. And makes *all else non-existent* for all practical purposes. If you appear in no search engine, you cease to exist. This is the philosophic theory of online existence.

Because there is no viable, national or international physical distribution for printed fringe literature, either as a book or as a newspaper, the internet in the only place to get fringe ideas. When fringe ideas are buried by search engines, buried 20 to 40 pages deep, few people will ever see a book like this one, or think about the ideas offered by a book like this one. We can almost believe, this is a deliberate form of global censorship, burning ideas too deep for most people to find. Current books might be easily available on lulu.com *but known to a worldwide audience of only 12 to 20 people.*

This is the reality of having Roscoe Forthright books on Amazon and on lulu.com ~~ **No one buys them if no one knows about them.** And no one knows about them unless millions of dollars of ad money is spent promoting them. Search engines are useless, for finding truly fringe literature. The fact you hold this book in your hand at all, is a major miracle of accidental propagation of fringe literature.

ENTRY #19

Entry #18 begs the question: Who cares? Why should any
bright Millennial, or any person of any age group, care
whether or not "fringe literature" is written or available,
or known to a large audience?

Roscoe Forthright would say, "Any person who gets all their
information, and creates their view of Reality, from only a few
sources, or even many "authorized", "mainstream", "college or
university", "expert" "mass media" sources, will *by definition*
have an inaccurate understanding of physical, social, political,
economic, scientific, religious and spiritual reality. All the
sources in quotation marks have their specific, and usually
economic, bias. Their information is issued to serve some
specific agenda, and therefore tailored to that objective,
designed as propaganda for whatever the current agenda
happens to be.

"Fringe literature" may or may not push propaganda, as it
offers *alternative descriptions of reality*, and alternative ways
of interpreting every topic discussed. Contrary, and well-
articulated views, are essential to forming accurate opinions
on any subject. To hear only one narrative, or several similar
narratives, leaves the impression those are the only accurate
versions of Truth. The loudest voice is rarely the truth.

Often the similar narratives can be all be completely wrong, and simply lazy reflections of each other. Those narratives being pushed forward while more accurate descriptions of reality get little or no air-time.

For people who are *OK* with superficial or inaccurate views of Reality, there is no reason for concern. Such people will go on with their lives, and do what they do, without every having one accurate thought about the large motion of society or politics or the growth or decline of our civilization. To such people the big picture does not matter. They are content, or at least *functional* within the objects and scenes immediately in front of their nose, responding to each demand for immediate attention. Day to day, with no long-term realistic goals at all.

Other people, prefer an accurate understanding of their lives, and the various forces at work in their lives. They want to understand political, social, economic, religious, spiritual, medical and scientific facts as accurately as possible. Most people live under time constraints, having limited time or interest or energy to sift through mountains of data, looking for accurate conclusions. That situation allows the pushers of propaganda wonderful opportunities to tell Big Lies, and get away with those Big Lies, and make millions of dollars from those Big Lies, before truth becomes known.

A work of "fringe literature" might clearly state the truth, ten to twenty years before the general population becomes aware of how thoroughly, completely and obscenely the con-artists did their work. As with Covid. As with Student Loans.

As with many things which come forward for the sole purpose of *moving billions of dollars* from the middle and lower class, into elite bank accounts. The continuance of the consolidation of wealth and real estate into the hands of the elite class (less than .001% of the population of our planet) has reached a sprinter's pace! This all going, while the rest of us are distracted with Covid masks, and every-changing Covid rules, and endless new inventions of social nonsense-- each and every one of those distractions, deliberately designed to keep us from noticing our losses of personal freedom, and our descent into total economic slavery.

NEW WORLD ORDER

...with several billion slaves.

Virginia

Open
Source
Software

Kim and Eva

Bea and Eva

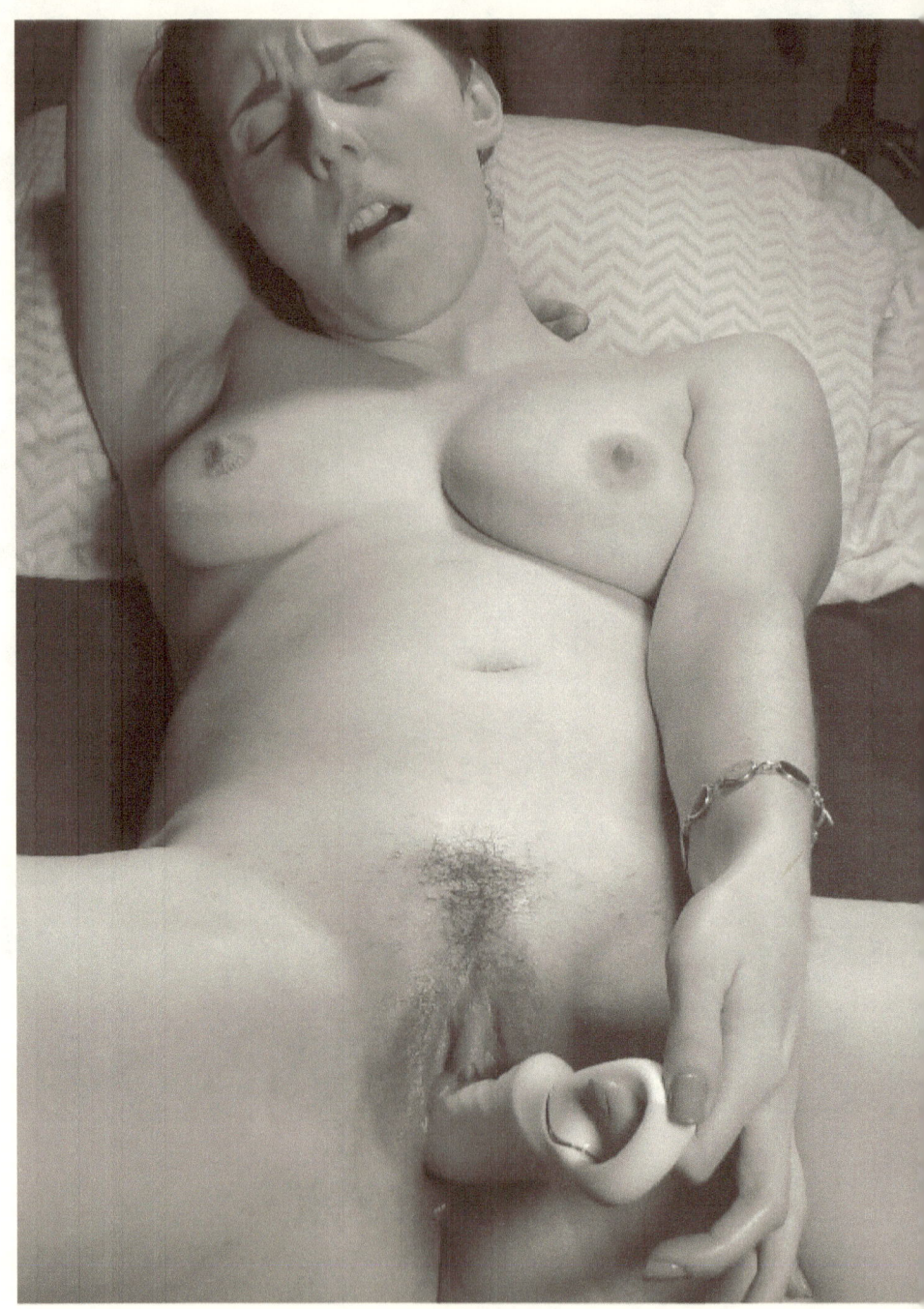

ENTRY #20

So what the hell do you really want from this book? From any
book? Do my thoughts and images exist for your brief, casual,
inconsequential, entertainment and diversion? Do you want
new ideas to consider, or are you completely OK with your
current sets of ideas and your current views of Reality? When
I say we are headed toward a NEW WORLD ORDER with
billions of slaves, do you think I am kidding, or exaggerating
the problem? Do you even acknowledge the tangible,
observable problem of global consolidation of wealth and
real estate into the hands of very few people?

When you are 60-years-old, playing with your grand-
children in a one-bedroom apartment (which is all you will
be able to afford) living under the rules of a totalitarian
government, will you wish you had paid attention to my
ranting, and the ranting of other "fringe literature"? Will you
wish you and all your friends, and your entire generation had
DONE SOMETHING, pushed-back against the oligarchs, and
retained your personal wealth and your personal freedom?

The playfulness you see between myself and my beautiful
young women is meant to entertain, but I am also sincerely
trying to get your attention, to get you thinking about the
larger and darker aspects of your daily reality.

I wish all smart people under the age of 30, would look more critically at the world around them, and not accept what they are told by "authorized experts" and political candidates.
In other words, the next time our government officials tell us *we are all going to die* from something like Covid, we need to say: "Prove it to me. The last time 98% of the people who died from Covid were already on the way out. Covid was less dangerous than driving a car. And, you, our brilliant leaders destroyed U.S. economy for two full years with propaganda bullshit nonsense."

Going forward all people need to push back against the bullshit nonsense, and hold both corporate and government leaders accountable for the destruction they cause. There seems to be a general attitude of apathy, and cow-like compliance in people under 30, *as if you all have no balls at all*, and do not have the good sense to stand up for your freedom, and all your other truly important human rights. (And I am not talking about LGBTQ bullshit nonsense as a human right. Those are varieties of personal bullshit, *pushed on all the rest of us,* as if those personal sexual quirks were relevant human rights.) The right to choose what vaccines go into your body. The right to choose where you work and where you live. Being able to afford good housing in a good neighborhood, having a good job. With good schools for your children. Those are relevant human rights.

Read a few excerpts from the *Tao Te Ching*, the Taoist classic by Lao Tzu, about rulers and government. Written in the 4th Century BCE, it astonishes *how little* our modern leadership understands about ruling countries well.

Good leaders reach solutions, and then stop. They do not dare to rely on force.

Chap. 30

If princes and kings were not exalted they might be overthrown.

Chap. 39

Cultivate virtue in the town, and it will be lasting.

Cultivate virtue in the country, and it will be abundant

Cultivate virtue in the world, and it will be universal

Chap. 54

Ruling a great country is like cooking a small fish.

Chap. 60

The supreme rulers are hardly known by their subjects. The lesser are loved and praised. The even lesser are feared. The least are despised.

Chap. 17

The more restrictions and prohibitions there are, the poorer the people will be.

The more laws and commands there are, the more thieves and robbers there will be.

Chap. 57

When the government is quite unobtrusive, people are indeed pure. When the government is quite prying, people are indeed conniving.

Chap. 58

To be brave without compassion, generous without moderation, and rule without refraining from being first in the world, creates many deaths.

Chap. 67

People are hard to govern. The rulers interfere with too much. That is why people are hard to govern.

Chap. 75

excerpts from the *Tao Te Ching* about Freedom and Free Will,
and the best use of both.,

A leader is best
When people barely know he exists
Of a good leader, who talks little,
When his work is done, his aim fulfilled,
They will say, "We did this ourselves."

The mark of a moderate man
is freedom from his own ideas.
Tolerant like the sky,
all-pervading like sunlight,
firm like a mountain,
supple like a tree in the wind,
he has no destination in view
and makes use of anything
life happens to bring his way.

The truth is not always beautiful, nor beautiful words the truth.

A man with outward courage dares to die;
a man with inner courage dares to live.

True words aren't eloquent;
eloquent words aren't true.
Wise men don't need to prove their point;
men who need to prove their point aren't wise.

The Master has no possessions.
The more he does for others,
the happier he is.
The more he gives to others,
the wealthier he is.

Love is a decision - not an emotion!

A good traveler has no fixed plans
and is not intent upon arriving.
A good artist lets his intuition
lead him wherever it wants.
A good scientist has freed himself of concepts
and keeps his mind open to what is.

Thus the Master is available to all people
and doesn't reject anyone.
He is ready to use all situations
and doesn't waste anything.
This is called embodying the light.

What is a good man but a bad man's teacher?
What is a bad man but a good man's job?
If you don't understand this, you will get lost,
however intelligent you are.
It is the great secret.

A great nation is like a great man:
When he makes a mistake, he realizes it.
Having realized it, he admits it.
Having admitted it, he corrects it.
He considers those who point out his faults
as his most benevolent teachers.
He thinks of his enemy
as the shadow that he himself casts.

Failure is an opportunity.
If you blame someone else,
there is no end to the blame.
Therefore the Master
fulfills her own obligations
and corrects her own mistakes.
She does what she needs to do
and demands nothing of others.

Roscoe On Eating Pussy

I ingest my joy slowly. Like eating a woman's pussy.
There is no need to rush. I savor the flavor. I savor the
texture of each pubic lip, and the texture inside. It is
much like a leisurely breakfast. Sitting in warm
sunlight, in a quiet room. On my plate are slices of
Bosc pear, slices of Munster and Havarti cheese. Two
soft-boiled eggs without shells. Two slices of
sourdough toast, spread with rosemary olive oil. Next
to my plate is a hot mug of Ethiopian coffee, spiced with
Arabic spice and cinnamon. I nibble. I take small bites.
I crush small chunks of pear between my teeth, and let
the juicy pulp linger on my tongue. I close my eyes and
concentrate my mind to the sweet flavor of pear, and
on the warm sunlight on my closed eyelids. Likewise, I
take a bite of Havarti cheese, and let it dissolve on my
tongue. I sip spiced coffee, and hold the flavors of
cheese and spiced coffee on my tongue. I take a bite of
toast, enjoying the crunch, and the softness soaked with
oil. I close my eyes, and enjoy each flavor and each
texture.

When my mouth is on a woman's mouth, or on a woman's vagina, I ingest my joy slowly. Just like eating a slow breakfast in quiet sunlight. My tongue moves in slow circles, around the outer edge of your vaginal lips. With lips and teeth, I nibble your lips, suck them into my mouth, and lay my tongue flat on your warm lips. I savor the flavor of your viscous fluid, as if the fluid was Arabic spiced coffee, mixed with the flavor and texture of soft bread soaked with rosemary olive oil. I swallow your fluid, as I would swallow bread, cheese, Bosc pears and olive oil. The sensual pleasure does not end with taste. I savor the clean, fresh, uniquely personal flavor of you. There are no scientific studies on how to change or improve the taste of a vagina. Some females rely on pineapple, kiwi, blueberries, mangos, and cucumbers to keep their cleanly scrubbed vaginae tasting sweet. Soap and water, and your own vaginal juices provide all the fresh taste and flavor I require.

When I spurt semen into your mouth. I want your pleasure to equal the pleasure I have licking your pussy. Move your tongue over the texture of my full cockhead, down the shaft; back up again.

Notice the roughness, notice the smoothness, the warmth, and the salty flavor as one drop off semen seeps from my small orifice. Likewise, allow your fingertips to explore, to savor the texture of my smooth-shaven balls. Enjoy the weight and firmness of my balls, as you squeeze them and caress them.

Squeeze my balls, slowly, deliberately, with my full cock in your mouth. Now, prepare yourself. You hear my panting breath. You know I will come soon. Open your eyes to see me smiling down at you. Then close your eyes, as my eyes were closed in sunlight. Concentrate your mind on the full swell of my cockhead. You can feel the moment of orgasm, the sacred moment before semen gushes into your mouth, hot bursts into the back of your throat. You almost gag, in surprise. The load of salty, viscous semen spreads over, over your tongue. You lick my still full cock-head, with my semen coating your tongue. You suck my still full cock-head as you swallow my semen. Swallow every drop of semen. Lick and suck every drop of semen from my tingling cock.

Consider this the first meal of your day. A hearty, nutritious breakfast. I will make coffee later.

I will bring you Bosc pears, munster, havarti, and cheddar cheeses, later. The sensual pleasure does not end with taste. I savor the sound of your moans, your sighs and your whispers, as you prepare to orgasm. As my tongue darts and swirls in and around your pubic folds. As your mind fills with pleasure, for the full length of your arousal. I enjoy the sounds of your wet pussy, and the sound of your moans, your sighs and your whispers. Think about all these joyful things, as you watch me stroke my erection for you. As I am fully aroused for you. For you, my beautiful angel. For you, my beautiful love. Here. Here and now. My rush of thick cream is for you. Come with me. Come for me. Come. Come.

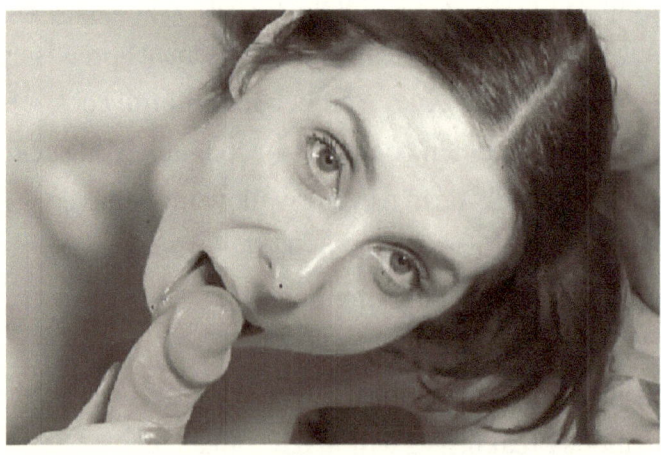

WHY DO YOU DO THAT, ROSCOE ?!

You offer philosophic quotes from ancient China, *and* *POW!* You are back talking about eating pussy!

As a thoughtful reader, I begin to believe our author has *several screws loose*, rattling around, with a tiny little attention span, popping from sacred wisdom to porn, and back again! In as few as six pages! And you just had to show us a young pretty girl with a cock in her mouth! Jeez, Louise.

How can we take you seriously, when you pop back to x-rated content, moments after giving us seriously good spiritual advice? Do you truly expect a reader to climb-on-board your modern philosophic spiritual bandwagon, and call you a guru, and buy your books and watch your porn videos, when you seem to have *no sense of common decency*, or even a hint of self-restraint when talking about your sexual proclivities?

And the Master responds: "Oh, my. You sure are worked up over a whole lot of nothing! I talk about what feels important to me at any given moment. And having sex with my cheerful beautiful females is important to me every day. I think about them much more than I think about ancient ideas from China, the Middle East, or sacred-robed Dalai Lamas in Tibet!

If you are looking for cause-and-effect, or clue to how my mind works, I will say this: I slap worthwhile ideas and human experiences *up against each other*, to provide contrast, to see if a reader is paying attention. Some readers just flip-through pages, scanning here and there, as many people now do on their cell phones. I would say cell-phones, in general have increased the short attention span of many people, and a *short attention span* now seems to be the "normal" way to ingest information.

Even smart people with good jobs, who have studied from textbooks in universities, and for those years cultivated long concentrated attention-spans, now lapse into flitting here and there like a drunken bumblebee, as if no flower is good enough, no nectar sweet enough, to be with more than a few seconds of personal effort. In this book, as in the first A-5, I cover many subjects, because I know people have many interests, and one long, cohesive narrative will not get the job done. The job at hand, as I see it, is communicating some difficult ideas in an entertaining way, to keep a Millennial audience within the pages long enough to pass along a few worthwhile ideas. The jumps from here to there, and on to something else, are deliberate. I know few people want to be lecture. I will be surprised if any group of readers takes in the full details of the *Forest Songs* and the *Twelve Necessities* from the first A-5 book. Those pieces seem too much like lectures.

I return over and over to sexual content, explicit sexual content because I know those words and those images have an innate draw among many people. I use those portions of each book to re-capture wondering minds, to bring them back into the pages, encouraging them to give a few more minutes, to look further into what this odd character, Roscoe Forthright has to say. I also rely heavily on stimulating a reader's own imagination, as they attempt to wrap their minds around the possible online and in-person group meetings, rituals and orgies involved in my 21st Century sex cult. I deliberately wish to keep readers wondering if this old guy truly has Sacred Lodges around the U.S. and around the world, in which reside willing hot, young nude women ready to teach Novices a sexual thing or two! A can assure you, dear reader, that is exactly what occurs from time to time, from place to place. Some of my books offer full details on those events. The A-5 books have an entirely different purpose. Here, I wish to cover more ground, with less detail and provide more room for philosophic and spiritual imagination to fly free. I am aware, many Millennials have never previously considers the sacred works of past centuries, as if none of those ideas, none of those forms of civilization matter, here and now in the 21st Century United States of America. The Tao Te-Ching, the Upanishads, the Bhagavad-Gita, the Holy Bible, the Koran, seem strange and distant to many secular American minds.

Being over 60-years-old, I have come to understand, those old, old, ancient book describe spiritual reality in much more accurate ways than anything being written in our place and time. The languages are ancient, but the human spiritual experiences are the same. The quote I offer from the Chandogya Upanishad is a good example. Written over 2500 years ago, the human experience remains the same:

"In this world they call greatness the possession of cattle and horses, elephants and gold, servants and wives, lands and houses. But I do not call this greatness, for here one thing depends upon another."

That is also true in our place and time. Our elite oligarchs *are certain, and live their lives,* based on the belief greatness is the possession of cattle and horses, elephants and gold, servants and wives, land and houses! Our wealthy elite, including most of our elected government leaders, are certain those things define greatness. Our elite expect us to admire their success in gathering wealth, wives and property. We are expected to want *to be like them,* to beg them entry into their grand exclusive world. And, of course, all that is deep, deep bullshit and nonsense. The writer of the Upanishads knew this over 2500 years ago.

With all this....

with every sentence and every image...

I am attempting an impossible task.

I am attempting to gently jolt sleeping MILLENNIAL minds *awake*....

AWAKE to a few harsh and brutal realities:

1. Your whole generation has been lied to by leaders of education, business, science and government, lied to <u>FOR YOUR ENTIRE LIVES.</u>

2. In the minds of the ruling elite, the OLIGARCHS in the U.S. and most other places, *the only purpose* for MILLENNIALS is to be useful economic slaves for the rest of their lives.

3. Your current and future economic slavery has only one objective: **Create more billionaire-oligarchs to run our planet**.

4. (Apparently, we need a few more billionaires to increase the rate of the consolidation of wealth among the ultra-elite, to decimate the middle-class and grow the lower class at a faster pace.)

5. Your loss of personal wealth, your loss of personal freedom of all kinds will continue for the next forty years, or *however long it takes* to turn the United States of America into a nation much like the current People's Republic of China.

    (Do not misunderstand. **That is the end goal.** Our oligarchs truly admire how China does business, and controls 1.398 billion Chinese citizens, while gaining economic control in many other countries.)

**to gently jolt sleeping
MILLENNIAL minds *awake*....**

**I offer images of pretty naked American
and Canadian girls being eaten,**

> **or sucking cock, or
> masturbating together.**

**Pretty, young nude women masturbating
together...** as an act of FREE WILL
is 100% better than the TOTALITARIAN
DICTATORSHIP OF OLIGARCHS.

Smart MILLENNIALS need to compare and contrast
those two forms of human activity, and decide which
one is better for the future of human civilization.

MORE THAN THIS > > > >

MILLENNIALS
need to get off their chubby apathetic zombie asses and do something about it.

Your generation helped make a

DRUGGED-UP dEMeNTED

SeNile Elitist Clown

the CURRENT PRESIDENT OF THE UNITED STATES.

(Are you really proud of that accomplishment?)

If you wish to remain FREE CITIZENS in a FREE COUNTRY, with FREE SPEECH, FREEDOM of TRAVEL, FREEDOM of THOUGHT, FREEDOM of CHOICE, and SAVINGS IN YOUR BANK ACCOUNTS

EACH young U.S. citizen needs to stop being a bobble-head to irrational social and political agendas... specifically the agendas pushed by the current LIBERAL DEMOCRATS in most Democratic State in the U.S.

When COVID was announced, and began to take over our lives, All MILLENNIALS
should have said,
FUCK OFF. WE ARE NOT DOING THAT.

Instead we got millions of bobble-heads.

That is the power of loud national propaganda.

OK. OK. OK.

Now you all think I am being unreasonably harsh
and blaming MILLENNIALS for many things which
are truly not their fault.   I simply wish to point out
the huge problem of being pushed around by
national propaganda which has little, or

nothing to do with
ANY OBSERVABLE PHYSICAL OR SOCIAL REALITY.

MILLENNIALS seem to lap-up the national bullshit
like vanilla yogurt, sip it like a latte, guzzle it like a
RED BULL for BREAKFAST.   No questions asked.

FOR EXAMPLE:
 during an actual deadly pandemic
**ALL THE HOMELESS PEOPLE
IN ALL MAJOR CITIES
WOULD DIE.**

WHERE ARE ALL THOSE DEAD BODIES?

The homeless tent-cities of Seattle are as lively as ever.

COVID-bullshit-covid-bullshit-bullshit – covid-bullshit-covid-mask-bullshit-covid- moron-**kissass, bullshit**-covid-bullshit-covid-bullshit-covid immunization card-bullshit-covid-**pussy-whipped, bullshit**-covid-bullshit-covid-bullshit-covid-**bobble-head, bullshit**-covid-bullshit-covid-bullshit-bullshit-bullshit.

Oh. Sorry. Did I have a momentary lapse of political-social-ethical-propaganda-nonsense bullshit? Did my little bobble-head get rusty from being pee-ed on for two years by our State Governor and now our DEMENTED PRESIDENT?

Did I not swallow enough of the KOOL-AID to reach maximum velocity toward Dreamy Democratic Party-Land of *We-Care-About-You-SOOO-Much* LGBTQ Unicorns and Rainbows?

Oh. Sorry. Sorry. Sorry. Now I am insulting under-served and down-trodden socio-sexual subsets of America, and I must be castrated, and told to
SHUT UP YOU WHITE HETEROSEXUAL MOTHER-FUCKER!

WE HAVE DYKE-BIKERS WHO CAN KICK YOUR ASS.

And, **FREEDOM OF SPEECH** IS ONLY ALLOWED WHEN YOU SAY WE TELL YOU TO SAY.

So kiss my scrawny, white over–educated well
– scrubbed North American anus, EACH AND
EVERY LIBERAL moron,,,,

**NOW, you've none it
ROSCOE FORTHRIGHT !**

You have used-up all your good-citizenship merits, and
will no longer be allowed access to the INTERNET, and no
longer be allowed to PUBLISH RAUNCHED HATE-SPEECH
PORNOGRAPHY, and **NO LONGER ALLOWED to
BOINK DELICIOUS YOUNG WOMEN** nor MAKE VIDEOS
OF YOURSELF BOINKING SUCH WOMEN.... and **BY GOD,**
IF WE CATCH YOU BOINKING ANY MORE BEAUTIFUL,
DELICIOUS, JOYFUL, FRIENDLY, CHEERFUL AND WILLING
YOUNG AMERICAN OR CANADIAN WOMEN---
BY GOD--   WE WILL KICK YOU OFF OUR CONTINENT,
and prevent your hate-mongering ass
from infesting any other CONTINENT.

BY GOD.   We have had enough of you
ROSCOE FORTHRIGHT.   BY GOD.

And, why the **L.A. LAKERS?** How did they get
into this book?

Well, Roscoe enjoys the NBA, and Virginia created
this weed-rolling tray in her art studio, and Roscoe
likes the tray almost as much as the NBA, and **Virginia**
has given Roscoe great pleasure for many years, and
why the fuck do you care anyway? You are only a
reader of this book, not the creator of this book.

Go create you own book if you want a specific reason
for every goddamn little thing you see here. Fuck.
Fuck me. What are you expecting from one aging
author trying to make a philosophic point or two?
I am no LeBron spanking down hoops.

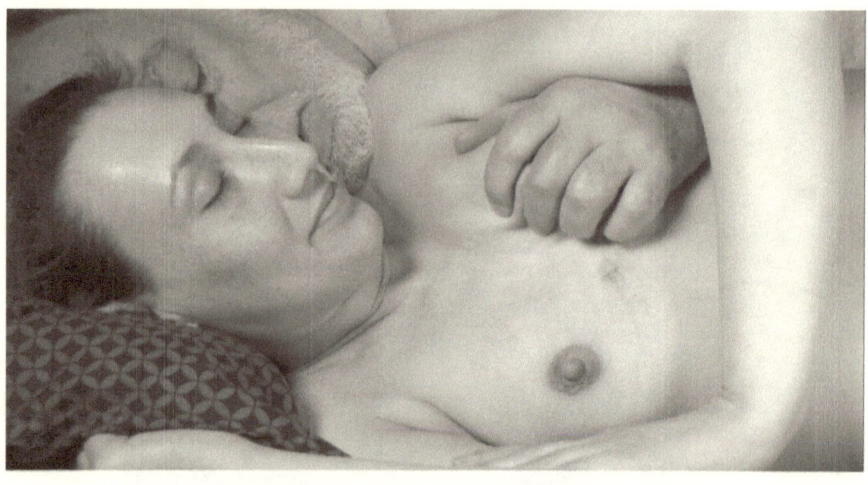

We move from the NBA to poets, famous poets from the 1980s.

Perhaps now is a good time to remember the poets who inspired me, made me think, made me consider language carefully. I paid close attention to a few poets in the 1980s and 1990s. I corresponded with William Stafford, and sometimes with Naomi Shihab Nye, W.S. Merwin and Robert Bly. These poets along with Pablo Neruda, Czeslaw Milosz and Marvin Bell opened my imagination to the subtle intensity of language, diverse ways to deliver a story, or a hint of a story, or the mood which precedes the story. Layered phrases of meaning with hints of further possibilities.

William E. Stafford

The first time I met William Stafford he was standing in line at the Post Office in Lake Oswego, Oregon. I smiled at him and said, "I recognize you. You are William Stafford. I have seen your picture on the back of your books." Being a polite man, he extended his hand, to shake my hand, and said, "Hello." Over a period of eight years, we visited with each other a few times, once at Lewis and Clark College, at several poetry workshops, and when I made videos of him reading poetry for a show I hosted on cable access television in Tigard.

One of the shows featured both Bill Stafford and Marvin Bell.
I truly enjoy what happened as we were setting up
microphones and cameras, as much as what we captured
on videotape. (yes, we used VHS tapes then.)

Bill and Marvin sat facing each other and held a conversation
about languages, the articulation and syntax of various
languages, including Native American languages. This is the
level of seriousness both men brought to their art. Both men as
interested in the sound and the rhythm of language, just as
much as they were interested in what any words collected
into a poem might have to say. They considered sound as
seriously as a composer considered sound.

After I moves from Oregon to California, Bill and I exchanged
twenty or more letters, often just news about our lives. I do
remember my last conversation with him. Two weeks after his
son died by suicide. I called him at his home in Lake Oswego.
He answered, and needed to move the phone to his garage, as
the house was noisy with guests. After a few words, I could
not hold back my natural response. I said, " I love you, Bill. I
am so sorry about your son."

There was a long pause. Then he said, "Thank you, Chuck."
I remember Bill Stafford as a generous man. Clear-headed
about what he could do and what he could not do.

Always willing to encourage young talent, and often more interested in young people and their talent and their ideas, more than in the works of famous writers. Except Charles Dickens. At some point he told me he was re-reading all the works of Charles Dickens. Our casual conversations covered many topics, including the creative process of Mozart, and creative inspiration in general.

Regarding politics and protest, he mentioned. Many student protestors in the 70s had no idea, the college professor with his briefcase and backpack full of books was close to their cause. William Stafford knew, occupying a campus and burning things would cause little significant change. He was as glad as anyone to see the Vietnam War end. He was also aware, this would not be the last war created by the leaders of the United States of America. And, as a paid employee of a college, he was required to remain cautious with what he said and did in public. We see this in his poems. Never raising an angry fist to shout righteous anger about anything. His anger was restrained, and written in calm, though sometimes frightening, turns of careful language. He was above all things among the most practical poets I have ever met.

21 May 87

Dear Chuck,

Just as I am poised to take off for Long Beach,
Washington, to read with Kim at the Shelburne Inn,
here comes your strong poem.
Maybe it will help me put more bite into my recent
products, which seem to be verging toward minimalist
Don't get too tough. The times are pickling us,
but we must stay human, I keep telling myself.
I'm off - -

Bill Stafford

W.S. Merwin

In addition to thoughtful and beautiful poem, W.S. Merwin
was supportive, giving strength to my artistic temperament,
during youthful moments of horror which leaned toward
suicide. He wrote to me, saying several of his friends
died by suicide, and the hole they left in his life was
inconsolable.

He understood my intense pain and disappointment with the economic of 20th Century America, artists struggling to physically survive. He said life itself was far to valuable cut short, even with all the suffering. Live through it.
Move past it. Create what you need. Those are not exact words, just the general ideas he wanted me to consider.

Some years later, when I worked for the Borders Bookstore chain, I made arrangement with the Public Relations Office at the nuclear submarine base in Bangor, Washington. I offered naval personal a 20% discount on all books, and specifically created book-lists, suggested reading to men who lived inside submarines. I was told each nuclear submarine has a paperback library, a locker full of books for the boys to read during long months at sea.

Not really sure what book to include on my book-list, I wrote to Galway Kinnell, W.S. Merwin and a few other poets for suggestions. I specifically asked the poets what books they would hope the man sitting behind the launch button may have read. Only W.S. Merwin responded with helpful ideas. He suggested *Huckleberry Finn* and the poetry of Emily Dickinson. He thought those would be subversive enough for any nuclear sub.

W.S. Merwin went further, to write a piece called *Undersea Libraries* which was later published in the *American Poetry Review*. I still have a photocopy is his original manuscript of that piece, typed on some old typewriter Merwin had in Hawaii.

Thinking about W.S. Merwin, other memories arrive. I remember how his eyes sparkled when he mentioned having several of his short poems published in *The New Yorker* magazine. For him a big win, a way to reach a larger audience than is usually available to poets. An average poet, on an average day, never gets to reach an audience of one million or more readers.

Naomi Shihab Nye

In the 1980s my she was my favorite poet. Her best work delivered a stunning blow. Someone called her the velvet hammer. After attending several readings and several workshops, of course, I fell in love with her. In two workshops, I was the only man present. I found this curious, and never reached a conclusion about why Naomi's closest followers were women. Overwhelmed, amazed by her beauty, intelligence and exotic creative language all inside one human female.

Honestly, I had never met a girl like this before. We had nothing like her in Escanaba, Michigan in the late 1970s. And though, I then lived in California with many excellent females with excellent talents, my imagination was still the imagination of a boy who grew up in Escanaba, Michigan.

And that was not a bad thing. I was different from boys who grew up in big cities. I understood the refraction of water, shooting arrows at carp and missing. Decades later my love for her and my love for her poems seems far less important. My mind has moved for decades further and further into music, and who I was, and what I felt, and what I thought about long ago remains useful only in how it drove me forward, to where I now stand. In the woods behind my house, listening to a wood thrush, thinking how I cannot stop singing anymore than the bird can stop singing. Sometime in the late 1980's I wrote this poem:

Naomi (an apple for a teacher)
She braids courage every morning,
lifts a guitar and sings:
I haven't given up.
Round rims frame more than I can hold.

On a pillow, shoes shoe to one side,
she sits and asks: What makes a man
with a gun look bigger?
C, D, G and e minor,
only four chords were
necessary for Thoreau.
Maybe trees,
nothing else in our world
understands the literal sky
defining white...
Clear as a yellow glove:
I haven't given up.
I never will.

Marvin Bell

One of several times I met Marvin Bell. Once, I hardly
recognized him, nothing likes the clean-cut photos on the
dust-jackets of his books. He wore a scruffy beard, a brown
fishing cap, and a black eye-patch over his left eye.
Just like a pirates. Honestly, he reminded my of a swash-
buckling pirate from some dark Hollywood film.

Other times, he cleaned-up very well,

as when I video-taped a poetry reading of him for Community Access Television in Tigard, Oregon. For the same weekly program, I video-taped Marvin Bell reading with William Stafford. I set a fern between them. We did that in the 1980s for Community Access TV, always a fern. I also brought along specific books by both poets, hoping they would read a few of my favorites.

On one occasion we discussed a few author who passed through Marvin's *Iowa Writer's Workshop*. Novelists and poets of all colors. He told me about visiting Thomas Harris's home, I don't remember where. In the tone of Marvin's voice, and the track of the conversation, it was clear: Marvin Bell the poet, and college professor was slightly envious of the creator of Dr. Hannibal Lector, and envious of the rewards of writing, *Silence of the Lambs*. No poet ever makes that much money for anything. Nor reaches an audience of millions.

Every writer has ambitions, and hopes they will be published by some company well-known for publishing this or that famous writer. One wishes to be published by the same firm which published writers one admires. Marvin was no exception to this human hope and ambition. On several occasions he was disappointed. Perhaps a willing editor left the decision-making role.

Perhaps the firm itself changed priorities. For whatever reason, Marvin Bell was passedover in favor of talented younger writers, and even less worthy writers.

I say this so younger poets will understand how the publishing business worked in the 1980s and 1990s. I have no idea if any *actual* publishing business exists in 2021. It is much like the record business and the music business, which both collapsed with the end of physical bookstores and physical record stores. To me, both industries appear to be *pretending to still be worthwhile.* They make as much money as possible from licensing the material they own to television and the movies. The book publishing business, the recorded music and "live concert" industries provide about as much opportunity for new artists as presidential elections provide opportunities for poor people. Only piles and piles of money buys one's way into those industries, and into those elections. Here I wish to mention another aspect of the *high-culture* industry in the United States. Artists of all kinds strive for seals-of-approval, from this or that popular venue. The NPR and PBS seals-of approval, gets slapped on the hind-quarters of a handful of writers, who get promoted on air and in documentaries. Those selected few reach an audience far larger than they would otherwise. One notices, the NPR/PBS approved writers are chosen to be popular with generally affluent white Liberals, and rarely ruffle the *generally-agreed-upon* popular talking points favored by that demographic. In other words, NPR would never let a person like William Burroughs on the air talking about his perverse sexual fantasies. Nor, Charles Bukowski's cheery and drunken memories of sexual adventures with co-eds on major college campuses. In other words, the NPR seal-of-approval deliberately limits the worldviews and the topics which will be promoted. Gay, lesbian and transgender angst is extensively promoted. *Heterosexual angst*, average heterosexual humans, being assaulted from all angles by loud and constant LGBTQ propaganda.... that does not get any airtime.

Marvin Bell once mentioned to me, the moral problem of being hired to teach writers to be writers, and poets to be poets. It is a recognized fact, one cannot teach people how to write, if the student has no inherent talent with language. It is therefore a deception to be paid to teaching writing. Both Bill Stafford Marvin Bell thought seriously about this moral issue, as they were both paid well by colleges and universities. Marvin say Bill Stafford solved the moral problem by gathering the students together, *to talk with each other*, to teach each other. In that many, he was out of the central position of hypocrisy.

Carolyn Kizer remains silent, and Adrienne Rich drops a pen.

When I asked Carolyn Kizer what made poetry *more* than a sophisticated form of entertainment, she was silent. Her grand-daughter sitting close by was eager to defend the art of poetry, urgently saying poems were inspirational, touching people's souls, giving people new ideas and comfort, and other things like that.

Carolyn Kizer remained silent. She understood the artistic problem to which I referred, and had no ready answer. Unlike Robert Bly, Carolyn Kizer was not ready or willing to say, poetry is a way of touching the Infinite. Robert Bly seemed to understand the ancient function of poetry.

Carolyn was altogether too American. Perhaps most everyone with a Pulitzer Prize does not wish to talk about God, and say their art comes from God.

At Black Oak Books in Berkeley, Adrienne Rich attended a reading by Czeslaw Milosz. W.S.Merwin was also present. I remember, after the reading Milosz and Merwin hugged each other. Adrienne Rich did not make herself available for hugs in that setting.

Without knowing who she was, I sat next to Adrienne
Rich in the first row of chairs. Later, after the reading,
Adrienne Rich browsed the bookstore, walking slowly among
the aisles. As I stood near her, she deliberately dropped a pen.
Took it out of her blouse pocket, and dropped it on
the floor. I knew my polite-courteous-male-response-
mechanism was being tested. She was being playful. Perhaps
she wanted to know if my Momma taught me to pick up fallen
objects for women. Perhaps she just wanted to start a
conversation. I picked up the pen and handed it to her.

But, I was tongue-tied, because by then I was fully aware she
was *Adrienne Rich* the famous feminist writer, who had
ambivalent feelings toward men, and truly preferred to
eat young, willing and cheerful pussy. That was too much for
a 20-something boy from Upper Michigan.

Here is a poem written sometime in the late 1980s.

Negotiating the Degree of Water Diffraction
The room you grew up in
overlooks a city, all the way to mountains,
as if everything were possible.
Where I grew up, I didn't know anyone
with a room like yours.
I woke at night hearing fog horns,
imagining long ship and salmon
moving through Little Bay de Noc,
and every night Lake Michigan
swallowed Orion.
At spawning time
I aimed every arrow low
to compensate for water diffraction
(*normal* is always negotiable.)
Wading to my knees to hunt
carp and northern pike,
in shallows killing for pleasure,
I made food for gulls.
Most things I've wanted are not possible,
not even between your flannel sheets,
wanting your love, moving once
inside you, and your heart,
your heart moving, how often?

Let us turn our attention to
Three Mystic Composers.

Cyril Scott   (1879 – 1970)

British composer, Cyril Scott, wrote a
book called, *Music Its Secret Influence
Throughout the Ages.* I own a
physical copy of this book, but the
book itself has no publication date. It
says only my book is a Third
Impression. The internet tells me,
Scott's book was originally published
in 1933.

Scott presents a startling idea:
Members of the Great White Lodge,
Ascended Beings, Devas with non-
corporeal form are responsible for the
greatest inspirations of the greatest
composers of Western Classical music.

Even, composers with no interest in occult or theosophic thinking, and a few composers who never heard of Ascended Spiritual Devas.
(Having lived decades before the popular theosophic worldviews of the early 1900s. Like, Beethoven, Mendelssohn and Chopin.)

The Hierarchy of Great Sages, Initiates, Adepts, known as the Great White Lodge, according to Scott, exercises mighty influence over the evolution of mankind. He argues much evidence exists for the Great White Lodge, and the associated descriptions of spiritual reality, *were not* the inventions of the much-maligned occultist, Madame Blavatsky. Scott says in his writings, "[In first versions of this book] I was indebted to a High Initiate of Esoteric Science for all my information regarding the hidden effects of music.

[But] I was not permitted to disclose his name, the time not being ripe, nor yet that of the remarkable seer who clair-audiently received that information and passed it on to me, to be expounded and elaborated. Fortunately, however, this injunction has now been rescinded, and I am able to acknowledge my indebtedness to the Master Koot Hoomi, who was my Authority for what was previously set forth, and for much added information which follows."

On further inspection, we discover there are serious doubts as to whether the person of Koot Hoomi, actually existed, as few people recorded meeting him. Most all his communications were in written form, and some have been confirmed to have been written by Madame Blavatsky.

Scott continues,

"His pupil, Nelsa Chaplin, a highly-trained clairvoyant of unusual sensitiveness, who since her earliest years had been in close telepathic contact with Master Koot Hoomi. She remember, for instance as a mere child, having been transported to Master Koot Hoomi's house at Shigatse in the Himalayas, where on many occasions she listened to those improvisations on the organ, which form part of His many and varied activities.

And more, "Both Master Koot Hoomi and the Master Jesus frequently overshadowed her and used her as their Medium. She told me one day, for the first time, she had experienced the wonderful sensation of being lifted out of her body by Master Koot Hoomi, and how, as she stood by His side in her spiritual body, she saw Him controlling her physical body, in order to speak to her husband and doctor.

Scott continues, "My own association with Nesla Chaplin extended over a period of seven years, and during that time, on many occasions, Master Koot Hoomi spoke to me through her, giving His pearls of wisdom and instructing me as to how I could best serve the Great White Lodge, not only though music, which He often inspired, but also by my pen. It was on one of these occasions that He told me the time had come when it was desirable that mankind should be enlightened regarding the esoteric effects of music, and its influence upon well-nigh every phase of civilization. "And it is for you, my son," He added, "to write a book on this this subject, with the aid of the beloved pupil, through whom I speak."

Thereafter, a time was set aside when Nelsa Chaplin would get into rapport with the Master, and while she clairaudiently listened to the data He gave, I would make notes, to be worked out in detail later. After I had completed a few chapters, I would read them to her, either at The Firs, or at my own house, while she would listen for any comments or corrections the Master might wish to make. In this way the book came to be written, inspired and sponsored by Him Who in a former life had been the great philosopher and musician, Pythagoras the Sage."

Hot damn! In our meek and unimaginative 21st Century, bounded by rationalist self-confidence, gene-slicing and advanced computer science, most people would consider that whole story a gigantic load of nonsense. I do not. This composer had no reason to invent stories and took no hallucinogenic drugs.

He was already famous and successful as a composer, and needed to attract no further professional or public attention to himself. I see this book as an honest attempt to do exactly what he says he was doing: channeling information from the spirit world, the Oneness, in his own theosophical way, doing what the Master instructed him to do.

I will quote further from Cyril Scott's book to give a further view of his thinking and his intentions.

From Chapter VI,
The Effects of Sound and Music.

Thorough-out the ages, philosophers,
religionists and savants have realized
the supreme importance of sound.
In the Vedas, said to be the oldest
scriptures in the world, it is stated that
the whole cosmos was brought into
manifestation through the agency of
sound. And, later on, the author of St.
John's Gospel expressed, in effect, the
same truth when he wrote: "In the
beginning was the Word, and the
Word was with God, and the Word
was God." The writer of the Book of
Joshua must also have possessed some
knowledge of the power of sound,
otherwise it is unlikely he would have
written the story of the Fall of Jericho.

"Musical training," writes Plato, "is a
more potent instrument than any
other, because rhythm and harmony
find their way into the inward places
of the soul, on which they mightily

fasten, imparting grace, an making the soul of him who is rightly educated, graceful." Plato's opinion of the effects of music are expressed in another part of *Republic*, where he says, "The introduction of a new kind of music must be shunned as imperiling the whole State; since styles of music are never disturbed without affecting the most important political institutions.

[We can hardly say this of our political institutions. The pervasive spread of rap music neither enhanced nor diminished the ridiculous choices made by our Federal Government over the past forty years! Our elected leaders are, by all appearances, tone deaf to any and all forms of music.]

Aristotle wrote: "Emotions of any kind are produced by melody and rhythm; therefore, by music a man becomes accustomed to feeling the right emotions; music has thus the power to form character, and the various kinds of music based on various modes, may be distinguished by their effects on character.

One, for example, working in the direction of melancholy, another of effeminacy; another encouraging abandonment, another self-control, another enthusiasm, and so on.

We propose, in fact, to show that each specific type of music has exercised a pronounced effect on history, on morals and on culture; that music, however horrifying this statement may appear to the orthodox, is a more potent force in the molding of character than religious creeds, precepts or moral philosophies; tor altogether these latter shoe the desirability of certain qualities, it is music which facilitates their acquisition.

Scott says this of Alexandre Scriabin:
"He was the first European composer
who combined a theoretical
knowledge of occultism with the tonal
art. Scriabin knew that he had a
spiritual message to convey to the
world, and that trough music it could
be given; he did not believe in *l'art
pour l'art*; such a conception failed to
appeal to his mystic temperament; he
wanted to benefit the human race, and
it was this aspiration which impelled
him to confess that the day on which
his *chef d'oeuvre* could be produced,
would be the happiest day of his life.

This *chef d'oeuvre* was to be called a
Misterium, and at it perfecting Sciabin
aimed during his last fifteen years of
life. Not only calculated to express the
composer's spiritual ideas, but to have
an actually spiritualizing effect on its
listeners.

Further, according to Scriabin, "it was
to have been delivered in the form of a
service, that would consist of
combined and simultaneous appeal to
the senses by all the arts."

From Chapter XXVIII,
*Music and the Character of the
Ancient Egyptians,*

We now come to deal with the effect
of music on the Egyptians, and the part
music played in their mighty
civilization. For if we have treated
Indian music first in order, it is not
because it was the most ancient, but
because it was the most subtle. Our
intention being to proceed from subtle
to gros, from the quarter-tone to the
third tone, and finally to the half-tone.

It was the third-tone which characterized the music of Egypt, and so rendered it one degree less subtle than music of India, with the result the music, instead of working on the mind, stopped short at the emotions. When the mind is spiritualized, it becomes the instrument of Wisdom. With the third-tone in Egypt, the music was intended to calm the emotional organism, to purge it of grosser vibrations. Also, in certain circumstances, the third-tone induced a specific form of trance.

An examination of ancient religions reveals the fact, schools for study of Esotericism existed (and still do exist) in every civilization worthy of the name. Schools in which the pupi; was taught not only the finer element of Nature, but actually to know them, to experience them. In Egypt these esoteric schools were called, The Mysteries, and in one of their most important ceremonies of initiation, the candidate, with the aid of music and other rites, moved into a form of trance. From which he emerged with a knowledge of the post-mortem existence. For the third-tone under ritual circumstances tended to loosen the emotional body from the physical body, and so induce *astral trance.* Through this experience, h learned from actual experience that he was immortal.

The Egyptians regarded music as having a divine origin. They held that harmony of various instruments had been discovered and invented by the gods. Thus, according to them, Hermes discovered the principle of voice and sounds, and was the inventor of the lyre, as well as an early form of the guitar. Osiris invented the flute. These suppositions are not at variance with the esoteric side of Egyptian religion, for before designated as god, these inventors were men, Adepts, great King-Initiates who walked the earth and ruled people. It was by virtue of them being great rulers, that they were deified. Much as the founder of Christianity was deified, and his disciples canonized.

The Egyptians did not trust knowledge of The Mysteries (and that fact their gods had once been men) to just anyone, reserving sacred knowledge to the heir-apparent to the throne, and for worthy priests who excelled in virtue and wisdom. The fact of multiple individual gods was much like the Vedic tradition of dividing One Consciousness, One God, into His many attributes. He would be called the creator of Divine Goodness, Wisdom, Power over the Earth, and so forth. The separate figures were never intended to be looked upon as real personages. They were symbols, and nothing more.

The Egyptian religion in it pure and
pristine state, before later denigrations,
was as exalted and philosophical as
the Vedic religion; its fundamental
doctrine being the Unity of God.
Given this understanding, we must
ask: If their music and religion, what
was lacking? What led to selfishness
and superstition, which brought the
downfall of the Egyptian civilization?

Egypt fell because it had concrete
knowledge, but not spiritual wisdom.
For knowledge gives power, and
power all too often engenders *love of
power*. Then, *love of personal power*,
selfishness with its inevitable
consequence, disintegration of the
community. When each individual is
trying to gain ascendency over his
neighbor, instead of co-operating with
his neighbor.
(Does all this sound familiar in 21st
Century corporate America? And the
polarized Government of the United
States of America?)

In the end, the Egyptians were entirely lacking in the wisdom-inspiring aspects of education, both secular and spiritual education. Its harmonic or divine aspect was too limited, and Egypt went to its doom, as did Greece and Rome after it. Much as in 1914, when the nations of Europe, because they likewise lacked wisdom, prostituted scientific knowledge to create a brutal War, the Egyptian had prostituted their occult knowledge. In ancient Egypt, simultaneous with the ethical decline, music began to deteriorate, and the small amount of harmony it once had disappeared.

The evil began in the priesthood. As already said, many of the priests had at one time been initiated into The Mysteries, but over a course of years, fewer and fewer were found worthy of that honor. Egoism and a fondness for power began to take over.

The love of beauty, truth and the higher emotions decreased, together with their love of music, music being the medium through which higher emotions were expressed. The priests grew indifferent and careless of how the sacred music was rendered, and eventually diluted the standard ritual music with extraneous music. The exulted influence of sacred music was withdrawn, and the character of both the priests and the people degenerated. With the little knowledge remaining, which had filtered through the lesser Mysteries, much of the true significance had been forgotten, and the priests worked on the minds of the people, paralyzing their reasoning powers,the result being, the Egyptians gave way to the grossest superstitions. In truth, the priests subjugated occult forces for evil ends, the acquisition of personal power over tens of thousands of people.

When a nation resorts to this, its doom
is inevitable. (Does all this sound
familiar in 21st Century deliberately,
egotistically, politically divided
America? And in five or six decades of
deception, among the initiated clergy
of the Catholic Church?)

portrait of Dane Rudhyar

Dane Rudhyar   (1895 – 1985)

French composer, occult theosophist, astrologer and writer, Dane Rudhyar was born Daniel Chennevière in Paris in 1895. Rudhyar emigrated to the U.S. in 1916, spending the decade of his life, south of San Francisco.

Rudhyar's cosmic and worldview was very similar to my own, sharing my understanding of Oneness, Universal Oneness, and the Divine Intentions of the Universe Itself. He wrote of these occult beliefs in many ways, in far more detail, with far greater knowledge than myself. He had a thorough knowledge of ancient and modern astrology, as well as other occult sciences. I feel closer to the views of Dane Rudhyar than to those of Cyril Scott, because Scott relies heavily on the influence of *Ascended Beings*, Divas, Members of the Great White Lodge urging humanity forward, steering the course of human civilization, through music, and by many other means.

Dane Rudhyar stresses the importance of human interaction with Oneness Itself, direct contact with the Divine Intentions of the Universe. Divine Intentions being the operative force behind all great music, and all artistic and scientific inspiration. Oneness is what I have personally experienced. Unlike, Cyril Scott, I have no Koot Hoomi, off in the Himalayas, nor direct contact with any other Enlightened Beings.

I now offer some quotations from Dane Rudhyar's book, *The Practice of Astrology*, published in the Netherlands in 1968.

Astrology, as known by this writer, is shown to have been from the dawn of human civilization, the result of man's attempt to understand the apparent confusion and chaos of his life-experiences y referring them to the ordered patterns of cyclic activity which he discovers in the sky.   A man learns to identify his his consciousness and will with the "celestial" patterns and rhythms. He becomes one with the principles of universal order, which many call "God." (or Oneness) And living an ordered life he becomes an integrated person: a man of wisdom. Though the energies of his own nature or of society at war may beat upon his consciousness through the gates of his senses and his feelings, he himself, as a centralized and integrated Self, is at peace. For, to him, even the most destructive storm has its place and function within the order of his destiny, or of mankind's destiny.

And by "destiny" he means: the complete whole of a cycle of living.

Astrology, in such a conception of its character and use, is a technique for the gaining of wisdom through the understanding of the order in human nature and in all phenomena perceived by man: *a technique of understanding.*

If the individual sees himself as an individual separated from all else in the world, and if his purpose is egocentric and unrelated to anything greater than his self, we have a kind of living which is negative, basically destructive, and purposeful rather than conscious. *True consciousness implies a deeply felt and acknowledged relationship between the individual and the universe.*

An individual unrelated to the universe is a fiction. No individual lives in a vacuum. Related he is – to a group, a society, mankind, the universe. If he is not fully aware of this state of total relatedness he cannot be called truly "conscious," however brilliant his intellect, his social cunning and his success. He lives in terms neither of true intelligence, nor of spirit. (In other words, in a perpetual state of self-deception.)

To live according to the "conscious way," the way of true intelligence, is to live in terms of one's essential place, function and purpose in the universal Whole. It is to will one's destiny; to become step by step the totality of what one potentially *is*. It is to fulfill the universal Harmony at the place and time one is called to act. It is to become, as a concrete person on earth, one's natal Sky. It is to do so, not only in a general way, but every day, at every moment, with the greatest possible efficiency, accuracy and purity of motive.

But, how can we ever be sure we are living in such a way? What standard of value, what frame of reference can there be against which e can test the validity of our acts *at the precise time* when we face a new test, a new crisis, a new problem? Astrology answers: "Consider the sky. Question its ordered patterns. Ask of the universal Harmony for an answer. Just as Nature has a cure for every ill, so the sky has a solution for every problem. Every individual need, consciously and clearly formulated, and stated with fervent eagerness, is always filled by the spirit, if the individual does not close his door to the spiritual influx and the divine message.

When an individual asks the sky for an answer to a vital problem or crisis confronting him, he thereby, intentionally or not,

signifies his readiness to meet the
confrontation in terms of "conscious
living." It should be clear, however,
that this readiness exist in an average
person who asks for astrological
advice only in a negative manner. The
asking may be done because
everything else has failed, or because
there is no logical and intellectual way
of ascertaining how events over which
one has no control will develop, or
because it is an easier way than to
study deeply the matter, or in order to
evade personal responsibility, or worse
still, our of sheer curiosity. These are
all negative attitudes.

The positive attitude might be
characterized as an attitude of prayer.
According to it, the individual seeks to
ascertain the will of the universal
intelligence with regard to the
particular confrontation he is meeting.

He does not seek to evade his responsibility, but rather to increase his responsibility by making it as fully conscious as possible by relating it to the universal purpose or "plan" of life, or of God. It does not lead to a blind and superstitious following of the answer revealed or suggested by the astrological chart, but instead to a new adjustment of one's efforts in becoming conscious of the purpose behind the confrontation, an of all the factors implied in the issues.

An astrological chart does not say: "Do this!" It presents a symbolic image of all the essential factors in any critical situation, an image from which purpose and patterning of these factors can be revealed, if the interpreter is able to see this purpose emerge. Sometimes the purpose, that is, the constructive directive or solution is very evident. In most cases, it is not.

It may require as great an effort of attention to decipher the answer outlined by the astrological chart, as attempts to solve the problem by ordinary means. *Horary (hourly or predictive) astrology is not a saving of effort or intelligence, it is a reorientation of effort and intelligence.* It does not make life easier, but makes man more conscious of the difficult turning points, at which he has to make choices. It aims at providing a universal dimension to choices, instead of a strictly personal and narrow one, we might say, a "fourth dimension" of the will, in which time becomes a determinant and the proper timing of actions and decisions on the background of universal cycles is made possible, even in the smallest acts.

Often a person seeking information from horary astrology is to close to the situation to interpret the chart's symbols and suggestion in an objective way, that is, in an accurate way. Thus the need, in most cases, for an interpreter, as a mediator between the universal intelligence and the confused or impotent mind of the enquirer, a mediator who should be able to focus in complete mental tranquility and detachment the message of this universal intelligence. Thus also, the value of commonly acknowledged principles and rules of interpretation as means to guide the interpreter; for the more the interpreter bases his judgment upon the traditional meanings rooted in the common experience of those who came before him, the more his mind is likely to become a steady focus unblurred by individual biases or argumentative attitudes of intellect.

In horary astrology the individual faces the universal; the part faces the whole. Horary astrology works because the whole acts upon the part whenever that part is in vital need.

Just as the human body as a whole
secretes instantly anti-toxin and
hormones to come to the help of any
cell or organ, so God (as a
personification of universal
intelligence and spiritual vitality)
always seeks to restore harmony and
health in every individual whom life
has thrown off balance. This divine
effort to re-establish harmony in every
disturbed individual is the substance
of "Grace." It is the Whole coming to
the help of every one of its parts.
Horary astrology is a dramatic
presentation of the operation of this
divine Grace. Every *properly timed*
horary chart is a celestial pantomime
through which the universe seeks to
impress a message upon every man in
a state of crisis or vital difficulty.

The real function of horary astrology
is to establish a state of relationship
between the universal intelligence or
divine Grace and the individual
person buffeted by cyclic storms or

repolarization and the baffling confrontations of experience. It is not "fortune telling" as an escape from personal responsibility and effort, still less for curiosity's sake. It is instead a sign of the conscious binding of the individual to the rhythm and purpose if the universal Whole, in which he accepts full and deliberate participation. From this Whole the individual receives understanding and healing, and the key to his many problems, *in proportion as* he is willing to consciously fulfill his function and his destiny.

Alexander Scriabin (1872 – 1915)

This Russian composer evolved his
own harmonic system, referred to as
his "Mystery Chord" built not on
thirds, but on fourths. To some ears
his writing became increasingly
involved, remote and rarefied, until it
became difficult for listeners to follow.
He began composing beautiful,
graceful solo piano piece, much in the
style of Chopin. In 1900, Scriabin was
drawn into the mysticism of Prince
S.N. Trubetskoy, with whom he
attended meeting of the Philosophical
Society, whose discussion impressed
him profoundly. Scriabin was
particularly impressed by Trubetskoy's
idea of oneness of love and God. Two
years later, Scriabin was drawn to
Nietzche's philosophy which made
him identify himself with the concept
of the Superman.

Over a period of a few years, his creative ego became all important. He wrote, "The external world is the result of my subjective spiritual activity. The world world is nothing else than an antithesis of my personal consciousness. The 'not I' which is opposed to the 'I" is necessarily only so, so that the "I" in the 'I could create' can create..." Also, along these lines, "I am the apotheosis of creation; I am the aim of all aims; I am the end of all ends, " a means of converting life into, " a kingdom on earth."

His vision was not only a new kind of music, but a new kind of *Weltanschauung*: a unity of all social, religious, philosophic and artistic thinking into a new system. "Art," he said, "must unite with philosophy and religion in an indivisible whole to form a new Gospel, which will replace the old Gospel which we have outlives. I cherish the dream of creating such a *Mystery*."

He wanted that *Mystery* to summarize the whole history of mankind from the beginning of time to the final cataclysm which he felt would come someday to purge the world and make room for a new race of nobler men. He wanted to use every artistic means at his disposal: dance, music, poetry, colors and even smells. He even thought of devising a new language for his *Mystery*, made up of sighs and exclamations rather than words.

Of the composers I mention in this book, Alexander Scriabin wins as being the most revolutionary and ambitious, and perhaps the most mentally unstable. Not content, as Rudhyar and Scott were, with asking advice from the Universal Mind, and following that advice, Scriabin built his entire philosophy around personal will, and purposes defined by his own ego. He assumed his creative talent and intellect were the only necessary components for creating a

Gospel for his imagined nobler race of men. As if the Oneness, the Cosmos, the Divine Intentions of the Universe, God Himself *had no say in the matter.*

As things turned out, his *Mystery*, the great work, survives only with a few pieces and a written introduction. The plans and imaginary performances and rituals, remained only within his own mind. In his writings, it appears he seriously believed World War I would cleanse the earth, and make way for his race of nobler men. Scriabin was certainly not the first person to invent fantasies having nothing at all in common with easily observable reality, and even very little in common *esoteric reality,* as in communication with God.
Scriabin might be placed in the same category with Alastair Crowley. Highly intelligent, highly creative people; people with actual mystical, intuitive and occult skills, who chose to build their philosophic ideas around their

personal ego. As if ego gratification, and ego creations where equal to the Will of God. "Do What Thou Wilt" is in fact a very good idea, when used with humility and a sense of moral responsibility to the rest of humankind. Used as a function of ego, it is just as destructive as any other religious idea used as a function of ego. That is, the idea can, and does, and will continue to create piles of dead bodies, and lifetimes of suffering for the people at the receiving end of abuse.

At this point, I should clearly state my belief: Oneness values free will, Oneness requires free will as the starting point for valuable creative action, creative thought, and all the components needed to create sustainable and worthwhile civilizations, especially those forms of civilization *we have not managed to invent.* Civilizations which serve the needs of billions of people, without enslaving one single person; civilizations which last two or three thousand years. So far, in recorded history, our imaginations have never reached that far. Only the physical Universe has systems which endure those long spans of time. The Divine Intentions of the Universe are available for consultation. Free of charge. All that is required is the openness, and clarity of mind to receive the incoming information. As I have said previously, this is the beginning of my process, in composing must piece. I lay out some parameters: approximate duration of the piece, perhaps the opening key signature and time signature, and general emotional content. Then, I open myself to the God Inside, the Divine Influence. I should say, the God Inside is exactly the same as the God Outside.

Astrology may use outside reference points, the stars and planets, but those charts and divine influence made apparent by astrological charts, are a separate way of accessing the same source of information, that is, the Divine Intentions of the Universe. Music composition, as I practice the art, is a personal and direct way of understanding a portion of the Divine Intentions. Not nearly as thorough and far reaching as the practice of serious astrology. And not as thorough and far reaching as some religious practices.

Unlike Scriabin, I am not ready to say, the *Arts* are the most effective method of unifying philosophic and religious thought, nor the only accurate way to describe cosmic cause and effect. Music is only one method for understanding our existence within the cycles of universal action. And it is an immensely valuable tool for that purpose.

But not the only tool, nor necessarily the best tool. It remains a fact, some people have little natural affinity for music of any kind. I do not insult such people, as Shakespeare did: "... fit for stratagems and spoils." I acknowledge the fact, my art is not for everyone. Other forms of spiritual stimulation are more effective than music for people with no natural affinity toward music. It is a waste of energy, to force art down someone's throat, or tell them they are stupid, or a hillbilly, when they show no interest in this or that form of art.

In an interview with Ned Roremn, I had to laugh, hearing Ned Rorem's complete lack of appreciation for the works of Bob Dylan. *Thirty years later, who really cares what either man had to say about anything!?* Bob Dylan certainly reached a larger audience than Ned Rorem, and provided hours of enjoyment to that larger audience.

Those are provable facts.

To me, Ned's snotty attitude about pop music, and Bob Dylan in particular, sounded more like jealousy, than an accurate assessment   of Bob Dylan contribution to Western Civilization, such as it is.

Here I am describing the inherent nature of popularity in any field of human action. People come into style, and several thousand people or more pay attention to what the *stars* have to say. And a decade later, most often, an entirely new group of stars have risen, and are promoted as the new geniuses, as if all the former stars and former geniuses have not only fallen from the sky, their ideas, art or insights are no longer considered relevant. Vast quantities of human knowledge and accomplishment are lost in this manner.

A reader will notice, in this book I have quoted very obscure books, by almost entirely unknown writers. Even the composers I interviewed in the late 1980s, are known only by a small percentage of classical music lovers. They were stars for ten to twenty years, and that was the end of it. Their music remains in libraries, and their names remain in music history books, but not much of their music is performed annually, or known at all by people under 40-years-old.

The only exception is perhaps, John Cage, the least accomplished as a composer, though the most enduring as a 20th Century pop star.

I am certain, my music and my ideas are no exception. To this date as a composer, I have appealed to and been recognized by *no large audience.*

My erotic films have been seen and heard tens of thousands of times more than my orchestral and chamber music. And I could really care less. The world is going to do, whatever it does. I am not a grand self-promoter in the style of some artists and their publishers. Neither my income nor my ego rely on what large music or literary audiences do or do not do. This book, and all my music exist, to be found and enjoyed, or not to be found at all. I will make a reasonable effort to make contact with an interested audience, and present that audience with my very best work. As with this book, I spend time, and much effort creating and organizing these ideas. Mostly as a challenge to myself, with some small hope, some audience will come across a portion of my art, and get something worthwhile from it. As mentioned in these pages, with the rise of algorithms, and the limited distribution of most all forms of art, our age has more available than any previous age, but most of the material is buried to deep for any large audience to gather around it. Large audience in the 21st Century, most often need to be corralled and driven like cattle, with specific marketing, to gather around any form of art, or listen carefully to any stated philosophy, or read even one worthwhile new book.

portrait of Alexander Scriabin

www.ingramcontent.com/pod-product-compliance
Lightning Source LLC
Chambersburg PA
CBHW020432290526
45785CB00002B/806